An Essential History of China

An Essential History of China

Why it Matters to Americans

WILLIAM JOHN COX

Copyright © 2015 William John Cox

All Rights Reserved.
No part of this publication can be reproduced or
transmitted in any form or by any means,
electronic or mechanical,
without permission in writing from William John Cox,
who asserts his moral right to be identified
as the author of this work.

Mindkind Publications
www.mindkind.info

Cover Image - The Goddess of Democracy
A 33-foot papier-mâché statue
was created by art students in support of
a massive demonstration for democracy
at Tiananmen Square in Beijing, China.
The statue was destroyed by the
People's Liberation Army on June 4, 1989.

Dedication Calligraphy - Peace in the Pacific
by Zhaoyang Cui - Beijing

ISBN-13: 9780985785086
ISBN-10: 098578508X

Also by William John Cox

Hello:
We Speak the Truth

You're Not Stupid! Get the Truth:
A Brief on the Bush Presidency

Mitt Romney and the Mormon Church:
Questions

Target Iran:
Drawing Red Lines in the Sand

The Holocaust Case:
Defeat of Denial

The Book of Mindkind:
A Philosophy for the New Millennium

Sam:
A Political Philosophy

Transforming America:
A Voters' Bill of Rights

Millennial Math & Physics

Table of Contents

Leading Characters · xiii
Preface ·xvii
Setting · xxi
Part One: Four Thousand Years of Dynastic Rule · · · · · · · · · · · · · · · · 1
   Ancient China · 3
   Early Dynasties · 5
   The First Emperor · 9
   The Han and the Period of Disunion · · · · · · · · · · · · · · · 13
   The Sui and The Grand Canal · · · · · · · · · · · · · · · · · ·17
   The Golden Age of the Tang · · · · · · · · · · · · · · · · · ·19
   The Glorious Song · 23
   Conquest and Unification by the Mongols · · · · · · · · · · · · · 29
   The Ming Dynasty, Its Mighty Navy, and the Great Wall · · · · · 33
      The Incredible Ming Navy · · · · · · · · · · · · · · · · · · 35
      The Mercantile Invasion · · · · · · · · · · · · · · · · · · · 39
   The Manchurian Qing Dynasty · · · · · · · · · · · · · · · · · 43
   The Corporate-Industrial Colonization Of China · · · · · · · · · · · 47
   A Troubling Matter of Diplomacy · · · · · · · · · · · · · · · · 53
Part Two: The Communist Dynasty · · · · · · · · · · · · · · · · 59
   Death Throes of an Empire ·61
      The Taiping Rebellion (1851-1864) · · · · · · · · · · · · · ·61
      Self Strengthening Movement (1861-1895) · · · · · · · · · · · 63
      The Sino-Japanese War (1894 -1895) · · · · · · · · · · · · · 64
      The Boxer Rebellion (1898-1900) · · · · · · · · · · · · · · · 66

Nationalism and the Republican Revolution · · · · · · · · · · · · · · 69
   Sun Yat-sen and the Revolution · 70
   The May Fourth Student Movement · · · · · · · · · · · · · · · · · · 72
   Chiang Kai-shek and the Nationalists · · · · · · · · · · · · · · · · · 73
   The Foundation of the Chinese Communist Party · · · · · · · · 75
   The Northern Expedition and the Communist-Nationalist
   Split · 77
   Government by the Kuomintang · 79
   Mao Hijacks the Red Army and Becomes a Bandit · · · · · · · · 80
Japanese Aggression · 89
   Invasion of Manchuria · 89
   Attack on Shanghai · 91
The Long March · 93
   Breaking Out · 93
   Mao Takes Command · 95
   Crossing the Yangtze · 96
   Fable of the Luding Suspension Bridge · · · · · · · · · · · · · · · · · 97
   Crossing the Great Snowy Mountains · · · · · · · · · · · · · · · · · · 97
   Internal Conflict · 98
   Crossing the Grasslands · 99
   Splitting the Armies · 99
   Arrival in Shaanx · 100
   The United Front · 100
World War ·103
   The Battle of Shanghai · 104
   The Rape of Nanjing · 105
   The Battle of Wuhan · 105
   Retreat to Chongqing · 106
   The Puppet Government · 107
   Allied With the United States · 107
   Mao Bides His Time · 109
   The Japanese Surrender ·111
Mao Establishes a Dynasty ·113

    Mao Zedong Thought · 114
    The Psychology of Mao · 117
    The Communist Revolution · 122
    Establishing the People's Republic of China · · · · · · · · · · · · 125
Mao's Insane Reign · 129
    Taking Control of the Nation · 130
    The Hundred Flowers Campaign (1956-1957) · · · · · · · · · · · 133
    The Great Leap Forward (1958-1961) · · · · · · · · · · · · · · · ·135
    The Great Proletarian Cultural Revolution (1966-1976) · · · 138
    Deng Xiaoping Takes Charge · 144
    The Death of Mao · 146
Deng's Moderate Rule ·147
    The Democracy Movement and Tiananmen Square · · · · · · ·152
    Deng's Legacy ·156
The Tiger's Pragmatic Rule · 159
    Jiang Zemin (1989-2002) · 160
    Hu Jintao (2002-2012) · 164
    Xi Jinping (2012-Present) · 168
Part Three: China and the United States · · · · · · · · · · · · · · · · ·179
    Changing Course ·181
    Threats of War ·183
    What Can Be Done? · 186
    The Failed Economic and Political Systems of
    the United States and China · 187
    Communism is not the Same as Socialism, and Capitalism
    is not the Same as Free Enterprise · · · · · · · · · · · · · · · · · 190
    All Governments Have a Duty to Educate Their People and
    to Tell Them the Truth ·192
    Informed Voters Must Make Their Own Policy · · · · · · · · · ·193
    Voting is an Inherent Human Right · · · · · · · · · · · · · · · · ·196
    The Power and Payoff of Freedom · · · · · · · · · · · · · · · · · 200
    A Peaceful Pacific Community · 201
    Making History · 203

Epilogue·····································205
  Democracy in Hong Kong······················207
  The United States Voters' Rights Amendment (USVRA) ······217
  Sources ·····································223

**Dedicated To
Peace in the Pacific**

Leading Characters

Notables in Chinese history often have a title, as well as personal, temple, courtesy, and posthumous names. Moreover, given the various dialects of the Chinese language, spoken names can and have been transliterated differently into other languages. The primary names used below are the ones most commonly used in the West, with others in parenthesis. They are listed in the order they appear, and the page number where each is introduced follows their description and period of life.

Yu the Great founded the Xia dynasty around 2205 BCE. (c. 2200 - 2100 BCE) Page 5.

Confucius, (Kong Fuzi or the Master Kong) created the philosophy of Confucianism. (551-479 BCE) Page 6.

Emperor Qin Shi Huang, (Zheng) The First Emperor, founded the Qin dynasty. (259 - 210 BCE) Page 9.

Emperor Gaozu of Han (Liu Bang, Gao, or Ji) founded the Han dynasty. (256 or 247 - 195 BCE) Page 13.

Emperor Wen of Sui (Yang Jian, Yang Chien, or Wendi) founded the Sui dynasty. (581-618 CE) Page 17.

Emperor Gaozu of Tang (Li Yuan or Shude) founded the Tang dynasty. (566-635CE) Page 19.

Emperor Taizong of Tang (Li Shimin) is considered to have been the greatest emperor in Chinese history, (598-649 CE) Page 19.

An Essential History of China

Empress Wu of Zhou (Wu Zhao, Wu Zetian) usurped the throne of Emperor Gaozong of Tang and established the Zhou dynasty. She is the only female monarch in Chinese history. (624-705 CE) Page 20.

Emperor Taizu of Song (Khao Kuangyin) founded the Song dynasty. (927-976 CE) Page 23.

Genghis Khan (Temujin) founder of the Mongol Empire. (1162-1227) Page 29.

Kublai Khan (Shizu) founder of the Yuan dynasty. (1215-1294) Page 29.

The Hongwu Emperor (Zhu Yuanzhang or Ming Taizu) founded the Ming dynasty. (1328-1398) Page 33.

Zheng He (Ma He or Cheng Ho) was the fleet admiral of China's greatest navy. (1371-1433) Page 35.

Emperor Kangxi (Xuanye) was the second emperor of the Manchu Qing dynasty to rule over China and is considered to be one of the most outstanding of Chinese emperors. (1654-1722) Page 44.

Emperor Gojong (Gwangmu) was the first emperor of Korea, who was probably murdered by the Japanese. (1852-1919) Page 55.

Theodore Roosevelt, Jr. ("T.R." or Teddy) was the 26th president of the United States. (1858-1919) Page 55.

Dr. Sun Yat-sen (Sun Wen or Sun Deming) was the founder of the Republic of China. (1866-1925) Page 70.

Chiang Kai-shek (Jiang Jieshi or Jiang Zhongzheng) was the leader of the Chinese Nationalist Party (Kuomintang) and the Republic of China. (1887-1975). Page 73.

Mao Zedong (Mao Tse-tung) established the People's Republic of China in 1949 and was the Chairman of the Chinese Communist Party until his death. (1893-1976) Page 75.

Wang Jingwei (Wang Ching-wei or Wang Zhaoming) Mao's Nationalist political benefactor, who became temporary head of the Kuomintang following Sun's death and later served as the head of the puppet government during the Japanese occupation. (1883-1944) Page 77.

Zhou Enlai (Chou) was the first and long-term Premier of the People's Republic of China. (1898-1976) Page 78.

Leading Characters

Zhang Xueliang (Chang Hsueh-liang) was a Chinese warlord in northeast China at the time of the Manchurian War in 1931, and kidnapped Chiang Kai-shek in 1936. (1901-2001) Page 78.

Zhu De (Chu Teh) was a commander of the first Red Army and later Marshall of the People's Liberation Army. (1886-1976) Page 81.

Lin Biao (Lin Yurong or Lin Piao) was a leader of the Red Army and People's Liberation Army, and who played a pivotal role in the Revolution. He died in a plane crash after his son conspired to kill Mao. (1907-1971) Page 82.

Emperor Xuantong (Aisin-Gioro Puyi) was the last Qing emperor of China, who abdicated in 1912, and was installed by the Japanese as the Kangde Emperor of the puppet state of Manchukuo in 1934. (1906-1967) Page 91.

Deng Xiaoping (Deng Xiansheng or Deng Bin) was Paramount Leader of China from 1978 to 1992 and was largely responsible for its economic revolution. (1904-1997) Page 95.

Liu Shaoqi (Liu Shao-chi) was Mao Zedong's designated successor who replaced him as President of the People's Republic of China in 1959. He died as a result of harsh treatment after being purged during the Cultural Revolution. (1898-1969) Page 110.

Jiang Qing (Chiang Ching or Madam Mao) was the fourth and last wife of Mao Zedong. (1914-1991) Page 120.

Wang Shiwei (Wang Sidao) was a journalist who was put to death by Mao for writing a critical essay entitled "Wild Lilies," which came to be code words to describe democratic dissent in China. (1906-1947) Page 121.

Wei Jingsheng served 15 years in prison in 1979 for displaying a Democracy Wall poster calling for actual democracy as a "Fifth Modernization." He was deported to the U.S. in 1997. (1950-) Page 149.

Liu Xiaobo is a writer and literary critic and a current political prisoner in China for seeking an end to the single-party rule of the Chinese Communist Party. He was awarded the Nobel Peace Prize in 2010. (1955-) Page 155.

Jiang Zemin followed Deng as Paramount Leader of China from 1989 to 2004. (1926 -). Page 156.

An Essential History of China

Hu Jintao succeeded Jiang as Paramount Leader of China from 2004 to 2012). (1942-) Page 157.

Wen Jiabao was appointed Premier of the State Council in 2003 and became caught up in the corruption scandal of 2012. (1942-) Page 162.

Xi Jinping has been the current Paramount Leader of China since 2012. (1953-) Page 168.

Bo Xilai, Party leader and Mayor of Chongquing (Chungking) was convicted of corruption and sentenced to life imprisonment. (1949-) Page 170.

Zhou Yongkang, Party internal security czar is presently in custody after being arrested for "grave violations of discipline." (1942-) Page 171.

Ilham Tohti, a Uyghur professor of economics, is an advocate of democratic rights for all Chinese people, including Uyghurs, Tibetans, and other minorities. He was convicted of separatism in September 2014 and sentenced to life in prison. (1969-) Page 175.

Alex Chow Yong-Kang, student leader of the Hong Kong Federation of Students during the Occupy-Hong Kong pro-democracy demonstrations in 2014. (1990-) Page 215.

Joshua Wong Chi-fung, student leader of the Scholarism group during the Occupy-Hong Kong pro-democracy demonstrations in 2014. (1996-) Page 215.

Preface

It is not that the history of China has not been written. Indeed, the Chinese have maintained an extensive and comprehensive written history of their civilization for more than 3,000 years. A compilation of Chinese history in the Eleventh Century took up 1,000 volumes and another in the Eighteenth Century filled more than 5,000 volumes. Two ongoing modern histories of China in the English language run to more than 16 and 20 volumes respectively, and even academic surveys of Chinese history are necessarily long enough to be daunting to many, if not most lay readers.

Given the geopolitical reality of the People's Republic of China and the disturbing possibility of a military conflict with its neighbors and the United States, what *is* needed is an *essential* history of ancient and modern China. People in the West, especially Americans and their political leaders, need accurate information about China's past in order to make intelligent decisions regarding the future of the world we share. The Chinese people require the truth about the government they live under if they are to ever achieve representative democracy. Both people must understand the hopes, dreams, and aspirations of each other.

Rather than a synopsis of Chinese history, this effort strives to present, as briefly as possible, the most essential and valuable information. The focus is on what is most relevant to the critical political and social questions that must be answered correctly and wisely, if war is to be avoided and peace is to prevail in the Pacific.

The first 40 centuries of Chinese history is compressed into the first part of the book, and the events of the last century are expanded in the second part. A full understanding of modern China requires an appreciation of what the Chinese people have created and endured during their existence. There are sound reasons for the Chinese to feel pride in their past and to experience pain and shame for the humiliations they have more recently suffered through the actions of other nations, including the United States.

The industrialization of China in the last 20 years represents a phenomenal success story; however, progress in producing consumer goods for export has not been matched with an expansion of freedom and democracy within the country. China remains tightly controlled by the Communist Party, and important events during the last hundred years are concealed from its people.

If the first part of this book was written for the American people, the second part was written for the people of China—who have a right to know their own history. The third part compares the governments of the two nations and provides answers for both societies. Much that is going wrong can be traced to political corruption at the highest levels of Beijing and Washington, DC; however, lessons derived from the examination can be applied in both countries, leading to governments that better serve the voters that elect them.

There is no question China is one of the greatest of human civilizations and that it is on the brink of becoming a superpower on the same level as the United States. Whether it replaces the United States at the pinnacle of political and economic power, whether the two nations destroy each other in a destructive war unlike anything ever seen by humanity, or whether they can learn to peacefully coexist depends on how the critical questions that most concern the people of both nations are answered.

The leaders of both countries proclaim the exercise of democracy by their people, and they both find fault with the political and economic systems of the other. The most frightening thing is that each nation is moving in the direction of what is most wrong with the other. China is being drawn toward unrestrained capitalism, and the United States is becoming a surveillance state. Unless the course is corrected, the inevitable consequence will be that the people of both nations will become enslaved by corporations. Should that occur, the elemental light of personal freedom and creativity in both nations will be extinguished, perhaps never to burn again.

The United States' relations with China, including conflicts over digital warfare and disputed islands in the China Seas, have taken on dangerous, confrontational aspects. We should find hope in the ability of the Chinese and American people to accept new ideas and modify their governments. An examination of the political problems the two societies have in common may reveal a peaceful path from the present to the future, which will be shared by the children of both nations and all who follow in their footsteps.

What is needed at this point in human history is not another violent revolution, no matter how valiant the cause. Rather, we must pursue an alternative vision of political evolution in which all nations, including the United States and China, peacefully evolve their governments to allow the people themselves to vote on the policies that most concern them. The people must use their inherent right of self government to elect responsible representatives to effectuate the people's own policies through the enactment of just laws and regulations.

The word "pacific" derives from the Latin "pacificus," meaning peaceful or peace-making. Imagine if you can, a community of nations bordering the Pacific Ocean, in which each country has evolved its own form of an effective representative democracy, and that all of these nations, and all of their people, live in peace.

(Image Credit: www. commons.wikimedia.org, Author: NordNordWest)

Envision that the people of the future Pacific nations agree on durable constitutions that define and restrict the power of their governments, articulate their human rights, and deny such rights to corporations.

The Pacific nations of tomorrow are committed to educating all of their people and to sharing the truth with them about all matters of government. Thus equipped, the people carefully consider and debate the social and political issues that most concern them, and they cast votes of wisdom in making their own policy by referenda.

The people of the evolved Pacific nations recognize the great responsibility they share for maintaining the common good, and they elect honorable representatives. Those selected by the people accept the solemn duty to implement the people's policies by enacting beneficial laws. Pacific voters physically demonstrate their power by very carefully and secretly handwriting the names of their choices for representatives on their own individual paper ballots, irrespective of any other option presented.

As all babies in every land cry in the same language, peace throughout the Pacific became the only choice of its people to still the terrors of their children and to ensure their future happiness. In the world of our dream, the people have firm and enduring control of their governments, and there can be no return to deception, repression, violence, and war.

If this vision of Peace in the Pacific is to be achieved, we must learn from history and shape our own future. With one-seventh of the human population on Earth and its longest continuing culture, the story of the Chinese people includes some of the most significant events of our collective history. We have much to learn from that narrative, and hopefully there is time enough remaining to make good use of it.

Let us now look upon the brilliant star of China, which has shone across the Pacific for thousands of years, whose people have lived and died under harsh rule throughout those millennia, and whose hunger for freedom can no longer be denied.

Setting

Geography, perhaps more than any other single feature, has unified the Chinese people and defined their relationships with their neighbors. The geophysical area of greater China is bounded on the east by the mighty Pacific Ocean, on the south by wet jungles, on the west by high mountains, and on the north by a dry desert and barren plateau. Two great rivers, the Yellow in the north and the Yangtze in the south, meander through this vast and fertile area, which is comparable in size to the United States, Canada, and Russia, individually. At 1.3 billion people, however, the population of China is almost double that of the other three nations combined.

Due to prevailing climatic conditions, the Northern China plain tends to be dry, lending itself to the production of millet grain in large fields that support farming families gathered in small villages. Because the hilly South receives much more rain, the people there grow rice in small terraced fields, which feed a much larger population.

Although people in the various parts of China speak different dialects of their common language, all Chinese use the same system of written communication, as do the Koreans, Japanese, and, for a time, the Vietnamese. Over the millennia, China has had a great political and cultural influence on its neighbors and, through its inventions (such as the magnetic compass and gunpowder) and economic exports (including tea, porcelain, and silk), on the rest of the world.

An Essential History of China

Living in semi-isolation, the Chinese came to view themselves as occupying the center of the world, having or producing most of what they needed and desiring little from outside.

This is the cradle of the Chinese people and their civilization. It is the stage upon which the drama of their lives will be played out.

Setting

(Image Credit: United States Central Intelligence Agency)

Part One: Four Thousand Years of Dynastic Rule

Ancient China

Based on DNA testing, we currently believe our human ancestors migrated out of Africa as early as 140,000 years ago and, perhaps, as late as 60,000 years in the past. Questions remain about the paths they took and who they encountered along the way. A set of undoubtedly *Homo sapiens* teeth recently discovered in a cave in Hunan province are believed to be at least 80,000 years old, which brings into question whether humans migrated through China into Europe, instead of the reverse.

We are not sure when or how humans arrived in East Asia, but we are learning that proto-human life had already thrived there for millennia. Beginning in 1927 with the excavation of a *Homo erectus* skull in a gigantic cave near modern Beijing, additional discoveries have established occupation as early as 780,000 years ago. Radiocarbon dating of other skulls found in another nearby cave suggests the presence of *Homo sapiens* at least 20,000 years ago.

Moving forward in time, we find the ancestors of modern Chinese grouped together in several cultures along the Yellow and Yangtze rivers during the Neolithic period about 14,000 years ago, as they began to settle down and grow crops. By 5000 BCE (Before the Common Era), there were villages consisting of dozens of families, who raised pigs and dogs, made fabric from hemp, and grew millet grain, which they stored in decorated pottery. Two thousand years later, they had already invented the cultivation of silk worms and the spinning and weaving of silk cloth.

It is around 2000 BCE that one of the most magnificent of all human stories has its beginning. According to an ancient legend, the Chinese people were created after the separation of Heaven and Earth. Their earliest rulers were a series of wise men, who instituted marriage between men and women and taught them how to control floods, grow crops, raise animals, trade the product of their endeavors, and care for the sick and injured. From these ancient wise men, the Chinese learned how to read and write, maintain a calendar, and make ceramics.

The last of these legendary rulers designated his faithful minister named Yu to succeed him. It is at this stage we find archeological evidence of the beginning of a series of dynasties that would rule China for four thousand years.

Early Dynasties

Yu the Great established the Xia dynasty. Evidence of its existence as early as 2200 BCE, and confidently by 1900 BCE, has been discovered beside the Yellow River. Excavations have uncovered large buildings and tombs containing some of the earliest known works of bronze. In about 1750 BCE, the Xia dynasty was defeated by the Shang dynasty, which went on to govern from a series of capitals until 1050 BCE.

The Shang dynasty used the scapula (shoulder blades) of oxen and turtle shells to divine answers to questions and to record the results. When heated, the objects produced cracks which were then interpreted. These "oracle" artifacts, some which date to the late-fourth millennium BCE, contain the first record of Chinese writing. Using approximately 4,000 characters, Archaic Chinese is related to modern Chinese writing, and the language used was similar to classical Chinese. The first written book was produced as early as 1000 BCE.

The kings of the Shang dynasty controlled the production of magnificent works of bronze, many of which were used for ceremonial purposes. Although the Shang people worshipped a number of different gods and goddesses, there is also evidence of the early worship of ancestors—which would influence Chinese behavior for thousands of years.

Under the succeeding Zhou dynasty (1122-771 BCE), there is the first evidence that the king was required to govern according to an ethical and religious standard. A history written during the Zhou period states the Shang dynasty failed when its leaders failed to govern properly and the "mandate of heaven" was withdrawn from them—along with the protection it provided. The virtue of the king was determined in reference to the welfare of the state and whether the people were safe and well fed.

The boundaries of the Zhou dynasty were extended by conquest and peaceful alliances into other areas of Northern China. These alliances were sealed by the exchange of gifts, which led to the diplomatic concept by which tribute was proffered to the strongest, who, in return, gave gifts of a greater value as a sign of moral leadership.

Although the mandate of heaven required a king to care for the well-being of his subjects, he retained the power of life and death over everyone. There was no concept of legal rights. The only legalism was that good behavior and acts were rewarded and bad behavior was punished—all at the unlimited discretion of the king.

There followed a period of several hundred years in which surrounding states disassociated themselves from the Zhou dynasty, and there was almost continual warfare. Battles were initially fought by the nobility; however, the burden came to be increasingly laid upon ordinary people as members of standing armies, which numbered in the hundreds of thousands. Military arts and sciences were improved, which included the use of armor, iron swords, and the crossbow. There was an increase in walled towns.

It was during this period that Sun Zi wrote *The Art of War*. He observed that a ruler was measured by his success in war, which was "the road either to survival or to ruin."

Among the many independent states was a small one in northeast China that was the home of an individual who undoubtedly contributed more to Chinese culture than anyone else. Kong Fuzi (551-479 BCE), or Confucius as he is known in the West, was exiled and traveled through other states before returning home. Recalling the golden age of the ancient rulers, Confucius believed there was a proper "way" for a king to run a state in good order and harmony.

Confucius began to speak about his beliefs and attracted followers, who recorded his teachings. These "Confucius sayings" became a standard of conduct for ordinary people, as well as rulers.

Early Dynasties

Confucius believed a superior man was not born to the role, but was awarded the honor because of his moral behavior and accomplishments. Education from books was important, but in addition, a gentleman had to learn for himself how to behave properly. Self-correction and cultivation was a virtue. As an early version of the Golden Rule, Confucius is recorded as saying, "Do not impose on others what you yourself do not desire."

Rather than a god-worshipping religion, such as Christianity or Islam, Confucianism is more of a philosophy or way of life, which everyone is expected to follow. In addition to worshipping one's deceased ancestors, great respect and obedience is paid to one's living father—who controlled all aspects of the family. He had the power of life or death over his children; if they disobeyed him, he could sell them into slavery. By the same respect, males dominated females; they could have multiple wives, and mothers were even expected to obey their sons.

Confucian philosophers articulated three bonds to guide society: loyalty to ruler, obedience to father, and wifely maintenance of chastity for her husband. Breaking these bonds was equivalent to treason and could bring the death penalty. Everyone had a rigid and well-defined place in the society, and everyone was believed to have the capacity to learn correct conduct by education, from the example of others, and through self-examination.

There were at least six major schools of Confucian thought, including that of Mencius, where the sayings of Confucius were analyzed and documented. These schools produced scholar-teachers, whose role was to advise the emperors, staff the government bureaucracy, and maintain the histories of the dynasties.

Confucian principles have guided the Chinese people for 2,500 years, and the philosophy continues to play a major conservative role in their lives today.

The First Emperor

Coming to fruition in the state of Qi in the northeast during the Fourth Century, BCE, a combination of events set the stage for the unification of the warring states into what would become the Qin dynasty. The Qin combined cavalry warfare, which they learned from their northern nomadic neighbors, with infantry armies and mounted warriors in hilly areas where chariots could not maneuver. In a major evolution of industrial warfare, troops were equipped with mass-produced crossbows, with basic mechanisms, that could be easily operated by ordinary soldiers with far less training than traditional archers.

The Qin were counseled by one Lord Shang (Shang Yang) from the state of Wei. Today Shang would be called a national security advisor (or corporate lawyer). His advice, as recorded in *The Book of Lord Shang*, was that might made right. To gain power, the king must terrorize and punish, and occasionally reward. Shang wrote "Law is the basis of government. It is what shapes the people." The king's job was to formulate and enforce the law. Shang encouraged heavy punishment for minor offenses, in order to avoid serious offenses. His primary mission was to establish the strongest army.

This powerful force allowed King Zheng of the Qin to bring other states to heel and his self designation as The First Emperor of "all under Heaven." He is known to us as Emperor Qin Shi Huang (259-210 BCE).

The Qin dynasty implemented Lord Shang's concept of legalism, which placed the interests of the state before the welfare of the people. In a rejection of Confucian principles, legalism resulted in a complex system of rewards and punishment in which people were placed in groups of five to ten households and made responsible for the conduct of all members. A comprehensive code laid out specific punishments for offenses, and a group was punished if it failed to correct and report proscribed conduct. Using the same system to organize, reward, and punish his army, the First Emperor used mandatory head counts to slaughter and terrorize his enemies. Prisoners of war received no mercy.

It was a period of magnificent achievements. The boundaries of the empire were expanded to include much of central China; defensive walls were consolidated into the beginning of the Great Wall of China; standardized weights and measures were established; uniform gold and copper coins were minted; a comprehensive system of postal and marketing roads were built, with standard axle-width for carts, and regularly spaced inns for travelers. Administrative districts were established under appointed ministers; merchants were regulated and trade was heavily taxed. A population census and register was created, and a head tax was imposed on all subjects irrespective of wealth. Land was re-allocated and irrigated by centralized projects, and there was corvée, or labor conscription, for the construction of public works.

Under Qin's rule, the written language was reformed, and the characters were simplified, equalized and made uniform throughout the empire. One of the great tragedies of the Qin dynasty was the destruction of accumulated knowledge, out of a fear people would "use the past to discredit the present."

All histories, except those written by Qin historians were burned, including classics of history, poetry, songs, and other documents. The only exemptions were books on divination, war, agriculture, and medicine. Confucianism was proscribed, and more than a thousand scholars were murdered.

In spite of its accomplishments, the mandate of heaven appears to have been quickly withdrawn from the Qin dynasty. The Emperor died in 210 BCE; his son was unable to rule; the people were exhausted by taxes and cruelty, and the dynasty fell four years later.

The First Emperor

There is an irony in the fate of Lord Shang, in that Emperor Qin's son accused him of treason. Shang was unable to find a place to hide because, under his own laws, no one would risk giving him shelter. His body was torn apart by chariots, and his entire family was killed.

In the chaos that followed the destruction of the Qin dynasty in 206 BCE, the palace records were destroyed by fire. Fortunately, not all books were lost.

The contribution of Emperor Qin Shi Huang to the future of China is enormous. His concept of centralization of power and universal standardization became the model for China that has continued for more than 2,400 years to the present.

The scope of Qin's achievements came to be more fully appreciated in 1974, when farmers in Shaanxi province uncovered his burial complex. The actual tomb is still being excavated, but it was found to be surrounded by pits containing a "Terracotta Army," consisting of more than 8,000 soldiers, 130 chariots pulled by 520 horses and 150 cavalry horses. The terracotta statues were individualized, with those of the generals being life sized. The army was entertained by a retinue of musicians, acrobats, and strongmen.

The dynasty left a number of legacies, including the permanent name of the country. Qin is pronounced "chin" and the word worked its way into the Sanskrit and Persian languages as "Sina" or "Cina" and ultimately into French and English as "Chine" and "China."

The Han and the Period of Disunion

The vast majority (92 percent) of the citizens of China, principally excluding Tibetans, Uyghurs, and the Manchu, consider themselves to be "Han Chinese." This is because the Han dynasty that replaced the Qin was to be so substantial and long lasting as to define, historically, much of what we consider to be the Chinese people.

A series of rebellions against the Qin dynasty culminated in victory by the tenacious King Liu Bang of the Han, who became emperor of China and founder of the Han dynasty. Emperor Gaozu of Han was also known as Gao, (256 or 247 - 195 BCE).

Finally, all under Heaven was at peace. Contrary to the violent style of the Qin, Gaozu offered a general amnesty and incorporated much of the Qin administrative machinery into his regime. He defended the frontiers and expanded the boundaries of his empire by accepting the allegiance of neighboring kingdoms. Gaozu gradually replaced these kings and Qin administrators with members of his own family and trusted followers.

Gaozu formalized the bureaucratic system he inherited and supervised it through a troika of three "excellencies," who oversaw finance, the military, and public works. Nine ministers were responsible for the balance of the administration. A censorate was established to monitor the other branches of government and to keep the emperor informed.

Eunuchs—who were originally used in the imperial harem—gained increasing power, particularly in the secretariat, which controlled correspondence with the emperor. Later, a merit system was implemented to recruit and promote highly-qualified individuals to positions of authority.

An Essential History of China

Initially contemptuous of scholars and Confucian philosophy, Gaozu was convinced by a scholar, who wrote a history about the failures of the Qin dynasty, to adopt Confucianism as a basis for the ethical standards of his government.

Known as the *Record of the Grand Historian*, a comprehensive 130-chapter history of the past 3,000 years of Chinese history was prepared. The accuracy of these histories can be verified by their references to eclipses, which are precise to year, month and day, and even hour. The accounts compiled relevant state documents, annual reports, treatises on approved behavior, astronomy, economic matters, and biographies of notables. Over the following millennia, the Record was to become the first of an eventual 24 "Standard Histories" of all "legitimate" dynasties.

Following a brief interregnum of palace intrigue after Gaozu's death, dynastic succession was stabilized. Two hundred years of generalized peace and prosperity followed, until the throne was usurped in 9 CE (Common Era), and the Xin dynasty was briefly in power. During this brief reign, slavery and the sale of land was prohibited, and all land was nationalized and redistributed.

When the Yellow River suddenly shifted its course—following the neglect of river defenses—and caused a great loss of life, migration to the south increased and a rebellion ended the Xin dynasty.

The Han dynasty was restored and continued for another 200 years. The boundaries of the empire were extended north into Manchuria and Korea and south into Vietnam. Marriages of Chinese princesses to neighboring leaders and the tribute system of gift exchanges was continued to help stabilize relations in areas where borders were more vulnerable.

Land was returned to private ownership, and an upper class consisting of landlords and a well-educated gentry expanded. It was an age of invention: the abacus was developed as a counting device, allowing the rapid addition, subtraction, multiplication, and division of numbers; gunpowder—a combination of sulfur, charcoal, and saltpeter—was invented; and the production of harder steel was refined by forging layers of iron with varying levels of carbon.

The Han and the Period of Disunion

Confucian scholars became more powerful and were able—through their interpretation of cosmic and natural events—to manipulate the emperors. An imperial academy was founded in 124 CE to teach the classics, and thousands of students presented themselves for study. Written examinations in the Confucian classics were required for selection into the civil service.

As Confucianism became intertwined with imperial power, the concept of the emperor as the Son of Heaven was more clearly defined. Functioning with the authority of heaven, he had the unrestrained power of life and death, which included the duty to exercise that power whenever the bonds of morality were broken. Thus, appropriate punishment and the practice of intimidation became as much of a virtue as moral influence. At the same time, the emperor's moral example required his officials to critically examine themselves, establish their own guilt, and administer self-punishment.

Commencing around 168 CE, a series of dynastic succession failures, combined with intrigue by the palace eunuchs, replacement of the merit system with the sale of offices, and the threat of Huns on the border, contributed to the steady decline of the Han dynasty. There were a growing number of serious rebellions by the peasantry, and although a Han emperor remained on the throne, actual power over the empire was divided among three generals. With the death of the last Han emperor in 220 CE, the dynasty ended.

During the next 360 years, China was first divided into three kingdoms. Then, following partial unification, there was a prolonged separation between the north and south. The southern dynasties established their capital at Nanking. At one point the north fragmented into as many as 16 kingdoms before being reunited under the Northern Wei dynasty.

It was during this time that Buddhism swept through both north and south China, and monasteries were established throughout the land. A unique doctrine of Chinese Buddhism evolved, which interacted with Daoism and produced a native form of meditation usually known by its Japanese name of Zen.

The period of separation was not necessarily destructive to the progress of the Chinese culture, as it spurred creative competition and innovation. It was during this period the magnetic compass was invented. Although first used for divination purposes, the device became invaluable for maritime navigation. The Chinese continued to perfect the production of steel, using clay for blast furnaces, coal for high temperatures, and phosphorus to reduce the melting point of iron. It became possible to produce vessels with thin walls, improved ploughshares, weapons, and even buildings.

The Sui and The Grand Canal

There was a period of consolidation in the north during the Sixth Century, until there was a single kingdom known as the Northern Zhou. Following a succession dispute, Yang Jian became king. Although a non-Chinese from a part-nomad family and raised a Buddhist, Yang Jian strengthened his control of the north and established the Sui dynasty in 581 CE. He became known as Emperor Wen (or Wendi). Claiming descent from the Han dynasty, Emperor Wen conquered the south with a minimum of destruction eight years later and reunified China. His dynasty was to bear the mantle of heaven quite briefly; however, it was a very productive time.

The emperor relied on the *Classic of Filial Submission* as a handbook for his administration of public and private morality. The book teaches absolute submission in a rigid hierarchical social order. He once ordered an associate to read it as a punishment in lieu of demotion.

Emperor Wen took immediate steps to establish centralized control over his empire. He brought the army under his command, and confiscated all personal weapons. An examination system was established, and appointments to provincial offices were made by a civil service board. Officials were closely supervised by frequent inspections and censors; they were never appointed to the area of their origin, and they were regularly rotated.

A revised legal code for both North and South more clearly defined crimes and punishments—including allowing the payment of fines and demotion. Collective responsibility among households was kept in place.

An "equal field" system allotted several acres of cultivable land to each adult male and granaries were maintained for bad times.

Wen died in 604 CE after 23 years of rule. He was succeeded by his son, Emperor Yangdi, who may have had his father murdered. One of Yangdi's first acts was a general amnesty and remission of taxes.

During his brief 14-year reign, Yangdi reconstructed and improved canals that were originally dug during the Fourth and Fifth Centuries CE. Mobilizing as many as five million workers, he constructed a large portion of what became known as the Grand Canal, one of the world's great water engineering projects. Covering a total distance of 1,550 miles, the Grand Canal runs from south of the Yangtze delta north to the Yellow River, and from there to the vicinity of Beijing. It is still one of the busiest and greatest manmade waterways in the world.

The canal system connected the two main east-west rivers with a north-south connection that allowed surplus food and commodities from the south to be safely and economically transported to the north through a series of canals, and it provided water for irrigation. Vast granaries having a capacity of up to 33 million bushels of grain were constructed along the canal. The system was made more fully effective with the invention of chambered locks by the Chinese in the Tenth Century.

After a failed attempt to conquer Korea—and in an ironic twist of fate—Yangdi was assassinated and the mantle of heaven was passed to another dynasty.

The Golden Age of the Tang

As the Sui dynasty deteriorated, a successful rebellion was raised by a general named Li Yuan, a northerner with the same mixed Chinese and nomadic heritage as the Sui. He proclaimed the Tang dynasty a year later in 618 CE, but it took six years for him to take full control of the country. He became known as Emperor Gaozu of Tang.

Gaozu retained the Sui administrative machinery, including the government's organization into six ministries (administration, personnel, finance, army, justice, public works, and rites), which remained intact into the Twentieth Century. He made further revisions of the legal code and revived the examination system.

In a break with the Sui, Gaozu ruled that Confucianism, as well as Daoism were pillars of the state, while Buddhism was a foreign religion. The power of Buddhist monks in government was sharply reduced.

As a result of palace intrigue, in which one of his sons, Li Shimin, murdered another son, Gaozu abdicated in 626 CE. Li Shimin became Emperor Taizong of Tang.

Taizong was to rule for 23 years, establishing a golden age of Chinese history. He is generally considered to have been the greatest of China's emperors and a model for those who followed him. Taizong expanded the boundaries of China beyond their present limits to include Vietnam and Central Asia into Kazakhstan. While the Western world was in the grips of the Dark Ages, China was the largest, wealthiest, best educated, and most powerful nation on Earth.

Disdaining superstition and celestial omens, Taizong was a scholar of science and a believer in rationalism. He established a comprehensive system of higher education and encouraged research and writing about the dynastic history of China. Large numbers of Japanese studied in China and returned home to replicate much of what they had learned, including coinage and games.

In addition to literature, Taizong supported the fine arts, and the power and beauty of Tang poetry has been applauded ever since. Although the art of ceramics continually evolved throughout Chinese history, it was during the Tang period that porcelain was invented. Using a white clay known as kaolin, porcelain can be molded into very thin and translucent objects. Although porcelain can be painted in many colors, the traditional white "chinaware" is painted with blue designs. The objects became a highly-prized export to the rest of the world—contributing to an early imbalance in trade accounts.

Taizong had the self confidence to endure criticism and avoid the abuse of power. He relied on competent ministers to run the government and improve the lot of the Chinese people. Local officials were evaluated by the censors as to their capability to ease the suffering of the people and to aid the poor.

Although he had empathy for those governed, and he carefully monitored the performance of those who assisted him, Taizong increased the distance between the nobility and the common people. He formalized the superiority of his imperial clan above all others.

Having extended his empire into Vietnam and Central Asia, Taizong turned his attention to the conquest of Korea, where he became bogged down in a series of annual invasions. Taizong died on July 10, 649 CE, having designated Li Zhi, his 20-year-old ninth son to be his successor.

Emperor Gaozong, Li Zhi reigned until 683 CE; however, his consort, Empress Wu (Wu Zhao) became the *de facto* ruler of the country when Gaozong suffered a stroke in 660 CE.

Wu was the ultimate schemer. Having originally been Taizong's consort, she managed to get pregnant by Gaozong and arranged the murder

The Golden Age of the Tang

of his existing consort. Wu continued to dominate, even after her sons succeeded Taizong and became emperors. She demoted the first, Emperor Zhongzong, in 684 CE and installed the second, Emperor Ruizong—until he abdicated in 690 CE. Then, she personally took the throne and established the Zhou dynasty. A secret police force was created, and anyone who opposed Wu was imprisoned or killed.

Wu completed the conquest of northern Korea and established a short-lived protectorate. Although she was unable to maintain military control, Korea become a reliable tributary state. Wu also tried to secure her southwestern flank in Tibet with limited success. Having developed its own form of centralized administration, a professional military, and its own written language based on Sanskrit, the Tibetan state began to encroach into parts of Sichuan province. In addition, the Chinese grip on the northeastern area of Manchuria began to give way.

In spite of her Machiavellianism, Wu was a tremendously accomplished woman, having learned to read the Chinese classics, write, and to play music. She encouraged women's rights and commissioned biographies of famous women. Confronting Confucian tradition, she believed an ideal emperor should rule as a mother does over her children.

Empress Wu was pressured to abdicate in favor of her first son, Emperor Zhongzong, who regained the throne in 705. Wu died later the same year at age 80.

Zhongzong continued to be the victim of scheming women. His consort, Empress Wei, carried on an affair with the nephew of Empress Wu. Zhongzong was poisoned in 710 CE, and Wei's son—who may or may not have been the child of Zhongzong—was briefly installed as emperor before (Empress Wu's second son) Emperor Ruizong regained the throne the same year.

Ruizong reigned for two years before abdicating in favor of his son, Li Longji who became Emperor Xuanzong. Also known as Emperor Ming of Tang, Xuanzong was to rule for 43 years—which were to be the most glorious of the Tang dynasty.

Some of the greatest Chinese poetry was written during this period. The first books were printed using carved wood blocks, including some Buddhist and Daoist texts and private calendars that are still in existence.

Painting flourished, particularly in the north. *Shining White of the Night*—which depicted the emperor's favorite horse and is considered to be the most famous of all Chinese paintings—was created at this time. The first model of a mechanical water clock was perfected in 725 CE, two centuries before such a clock was invented in Europe.

Tang emperors would occupy the throne for next 150 years, as the dynasty bore the mantle of heaven. The emperors were mostly competent. Roads were safe, commerce prospered, the Grand Canal flowed with the product of a prosperous nation, and poets and artists produced works of art.

Because borders were never secure, vigilant effort was required to defend the nation. Alliances were made and broken; increasingly valuable gifts had to be given in exchange for the "tribute" of surrounding countries. The Tibetans intruded from the southwest, and the Uyghurs were bought off as mercenaries to defend the northwest.

The government came to ruled by a scholarly bureaucracy chosen by examination and merit, and the aristocratic families became less involved. The economy became increasingly independent, as the government exercised less control over it. Most provincial governments were run by military governors, and the power of the central government was reduced.

Eventually, the country descended into anarchy. Corrupt officials and bandits seized power and rode roughshod over the countryside. Most of northern China was seized by non-Chinese; the remainder was run by warlords.

A series of young emperors proved incompetent, and both the government and the military were controlled by eunuchs. Finally, attacked from every side and usurped from within, the mantle of heaven was removed from the Tangs in 907 CE, and China suffered another period of disunity for more than 50 years.

The Glorious Song

It is impossible to express succinctly what occurred following the fall of the Tang dynasty and the rise of the Song dynasties. Suffice it to say the territorial integrity of China collapsed, and it first began to reorganize itself in the north, while the south remained extremely fragmented. The Later Zhou was the last of five dynasties that controlled much of northern China during its period of disunion. In 960 CE, the commander of the Zhou palace guard pulled off a coup. Supported by his troops, Khao Kuangyin proclaimed himself Emperor Taizu and founded the Song dynasty.

Taizu was able to fairly quickly bring other northern states under his control by creating a professional and loyal army. He convinced local warlords to accept valuable pensions, rather than engage in combat. He quickly swept aside weaker enemies and used generosity and compromise to overcome most other resistance. Continuing the same tactics, he was able to reunify most of China before his death in 976 CE.

Living a frugal life, Taizu wore old clothes and lived in simple quarters. His personal motto was, "restrain my own desire and care about my people more."

Taizu was succeeded by his brother, Zhao Kuangyi, who became Emperor Taizong. He obtained the submission of holdout kingdoms and consolidated his control of China. The Song dynasty continued until 1279. Following its defeat in the civil war with the Jin dynasty in 1127, the dynasty lost control of the country north of the Yangtze River and moved its capital from Beijing to Hangzhou. Retaining a majority of the population and economy, the dynasty—referred to as the Southern Song—survived and continued to flourish within its reduced boundaries.

Relying primarily on the doctrines of Confucius, the Song emperors served as models of behavior and administration, which impressed itself on those who succeeded them. To rectify what they saw as the deficiencies of the Tang dynasty, the Song initiated reforms that were to prove significant.

To eliminate warlordism, a large professional army that reported directly to the emperor was maintained. The censorate, which had the power to remove corrupt officials, was personally controlled by the emperor.

On the other hand, the civil service bureaucracy became more independent. It recruited people with special talents for posts that took advantage of their abilities. New schools were established, and Confucian studies were revived once again. Sixty percent of successful candidates came from families with no previous history of civil service; test grading was anonymous; and candidates with a commitment to serve the emperor came from all over the empire.

A national market was established using the extensive water transportation system to distribute the surplus of agriculture production and other commodities. Finally, the government made taxation more uniform throughout the empire and became more directly involved in the economy.

Farmers received low-interest loans to increase production and to reduce dependence on landlords and moneylenders. The equal field system was abandoned in favor of free market principles. Peasants were not bound to the land—like serfs under feudalism—but were free to move and to buy and sell small plots of land. To stabilize prices, surpluses in one area were purchased by the government and sold in another at a profit. Tea was purchased in Sichuan and traded for horses in Tibet.

Under the Confucian philosophy of governance, the role of the emperor, as the Son of Heaven, was to make decisions. A Song councilor defined what this portended for the longevity of a dynasty:

The Glorious Song

Although Heaven is high and far away, Heaven inspects the empire daily. Heaven responds to the deeds of the ruler. If he continuously cultivates himself and treats his people justly . . . then Heaven sends prosperity, and the Son of Heaven receives the realm for all times. There will be no misfortune and nobody will create trouble. If he, however, neglects the deities, ill-treats his people, and does not fear the Mandate of Heaven, there will be misfortune.

China's population doubled during these centuries and was fed by surpluses resulting from improvements in the cultivation of rice and early-ripening seed. More than a million people came to occupy the capital city of Hangzhou, the world's largest city, and it engaged in a value of trade that was 50 percent greater than that carried on 700 years later in London.

The entire period of the Song Dynasty was a time of great invention, industry, and culture. Using abundant deposits of coal and iron ore, northern China was able to produce more than two hundred million pounds of smelted iron each year. The Song army was equipped with armor and weapons of steel and used gunpowder to construct rockets, grenades, and assault mines. Walled towns and cities of the time could not withstand an attack by the Song forces.

There was no place on Earth that could compare to Song achievements, and it would not be until the Eighteenth Century that any Western country would reach China's level of economic development or centralized government.

Chinese merchants exported porcelain, swords, silk, and other textiles to the West and imported spices from the East Indies. Chinese financiers invested in joint stock funds to underwrite international trade. Operating large sailing ships with watertight compartments and stern post rudders to India and East Africa, captains relied on compasses and comprehensive charts for navigation. All this was at a time when galleys in the Mediterranean Sea were still being rowed by slaves, and it would be another 500 years before the Age of Sail arrived in the West.

The Chinese not only used the compass for navigation, but they used it to discover the magnetic declination of true north, and they used sighting tubes to fix and note the changing position of the North Star. A half century before Mercator, celestial star charts were created using a cylindrical projection. A "planisphere" was constructed to demonstrate a rotating artificial sky. It pivoted on an axis, which was tilted 23.5 degrees to conform to the true inclination of the Earth's axis.

While people in the West commonly believed the world to be flat, the Chinese measured the Earth's circumference with great accuracy and published books about advanced mathematics, geometry, and mapmaking.

The Chinese had invented paper in the First or Second Century BCE, and had been printing books using carved wooden blocks since the Eighth Century CE. With the invention of cast metal moveable type by the Song in 1041, it became possible to publish large numbers of books. These including comprehensive encyclopedias, a 1,000-volume history, technical writings, and travelogues. Works of poetry and philosophy were popular and widely available at a time when the *Bible* was the one of the few books available in the West—one which was laboriously copied by hand.

The economy was booming and—even though the annual output of the imperial mint reached an astounding six billion coins—a balance of trade deficit caused a shortage of coins in China. The Song solved the problem by printing paper money for use as a medium of exchange, backed by the deposit of metal coins. This was 500 years before the first banknote was issued in Europe.

The Song initiated the use of inoculation against smallpox 800 years before Edward Jenner introduced it in the West. The Song even invented the pound lock for canal systems later used by the United States in the Panama Canal.

China was on the verge of an industrial revolution, but did not quite reach it. Problems began to accumulate, and the dynasty grew weaker with time. The bureaucracy got top heavy, politics interfered with competence, opponents were denounced and forced out of office, corruption grew, the

The Glorious Song

professional military was replaced by weak mercenaries, rebellions broke out, and invasion forces from the north became irresistible.

The Southern Song had co-existed with the northern Jin empire following the peace agreement of 1121. The Jin established a regional capital in Beijing, which relied on the traditional Chinese methods of central government, including the civil service system, and taxation.

The Jin empire was invaded by the Mongols in the early Thirteenth Century and, taking the strategic position that "the enemy of my enemy is my friend," the Southern Song made an alliance with the Mongols, allowing the Mongols to overrun northern China. It was to be a decision the Song soon regretted.

Conquest and Unification by the Mongols

The Mongols are first mentioned in Chinese history books during the Tang dynasty. More than just people from the Mongolian plateau, they were a confederation of nomadic steppe tribes united by Genghis Khan in 1206. He proclaimed he was chosen by heaven to rule, and those who opposed him defied the will of heaven.

For awhile, it appeared the prophecy was true. Invasions by hoards of his horse-mounted archers spread across Eurasia, sparing those who submitted and massacring all who resisted. The Mongol Peace extended to Eastern Europe, Russia, the Middle East and ultimately, of concern here, to all of China. The Mongol Empire became the largest contiguous empire in history.

Genghis Khan defeated the Jin empire prior to his death in 1227—when his empire was divided into khanates by his descendants. The one who received northern China as his portion was a grandson, Kublai Khan. He established his capital at Shangdu, which is known in the west as Zanadu.

One of Kublai's Chinese advisors told him, "although the empire has been conquered on horseback, it cannot be administered on horseback," and the decision was made to utilize the Chinese method of central administration. Kublai adopted a Chinese reign name and proclaimed the Yuan dynasty.

Turning on their ally, the Southern Song, the Mongols attacked the major city of Xiangyan on the Han River in 1268. Although the Chinese produced large numbers of gunpowder weapons in the war, the Moguls had also learned the technology. This was the first war in which both sides used explosives. The fall of Xiangyan cleared the approach to the Yangtze valley. Following the annihilation of a large Chinese army, the last of the Song forces were defeated at sea in 1279.

The Mongols considered themselves be universal rulers, and they united groups of people from different cultures and religions—both for administrative and economic purposes. With their conquest of Central Asia, the Silk Road was freely traveled by merchants, Catholic priests and Western adventurers, including Marco Polo.

Kublai was a Buddhist, and he appointed a Tibetan monk as his advisor, whom he assigned to oversee all Buddhist clergy. In return, Kublai was acclaimed the universal emperor in the Buddhist custom. The Mongol emperors placed Muslims from Uyghur in positions of high authority, providing a buffer between the Mongols and Chinese. Muslims received special privileges, including the right to be tried in their own religious courts. In grading people into a formal hierarchy for purposes of holding office, the Yuan placed themselves first, and then placed the Uyguers and other "colored eyes" people of the northwest over the Han Chinese.

Succession in the Mongol Empire relied on a political and military council to evaluate potential heirs, while the succession of Chinese emperors traditionally went to the eldest son. Kublai's two sons predeceased him and, on his death in 1294, there was a contest between his favored grandson, Temür, and his older brother. A council decided for Temür, who became Emperor Chengzon of Yuan.

The Yuan dynasty did not last 100 years, but by adopting the Chinese method of administration (including the six ministries, secretariat, and censorial organization) and following traditional ceremonial and Confucian rites, it found a place in the list of Chinese dynasties.

Some good came out of the Mongol conquest. Principally, it served to unite all of China for the first time in 400 years, and the Chinese people were somewhat left alone. By replacing court officials with Uyghurs and other outsiders, many well-educated scholars had the leisure to write and

Conquest and Unification by the Mongols

reflect on the past and future. Great paintings and works of drama were produced, as well as treatises on Confucian philosophies.

The Yuan engaged in massive public works, including construction of a second Grand Canal system, a magnificent summer marble palace in Shangdu, and a new capital near modern Beijing. To help pay for its military campaigns and these expensive enterprises, the Yuan increased the supply of paper money—without properly backing it with coin—ultimately making it worthless.

A series of destructive floods and deadly tornados washed across China in the mid Fourteenth Century, with a great loss of life and property. These "dragons from the clouds" portended the end of the Yuan dynasty.

As the economy declined, a combination of events led to rebellions, particularly in the south, and to a decrease in the ability of the Mongols to resist. The Chinese resented being forced to work on public projects for the Mongols; there was a rise in piracy, which interfered with the shipment of food from the south to the north; and local warlords raised militias.

The Yuan's ability to militarily quell the rebellions had decreased over time. Mongol soldiers had been provided with land in China, but found it difficult or impossible to earn a living. Many became impoverished and could no longer provide military service. The active military was poorly paid and became disillusioned.

As the wildfires of rebellion spread, they were fanned by religious and patriotic fanaticism. Widespread discontent, combined with a mishmash of religious ideas including purification, enlightenment, and redemption by the coming of the future Buddha, led to the growth of the White Lotus Society—a movement for independence from Mongol rule. Wearing red turbans for common identification, they began to attract attention and recruits, one of whom was a young man named Zhu Yuanzhang, who joined the movement in 1352.

The Ming Dynasty, Its Mighty Navy, and the Great Wall

Zhu Yuanzhang was orphaned when his parents died in the famine of 1344, and he became a street beggar to survive. He receiving some schooling—after taking refuge in a Buddhist temple—before becoming a soldier. With military training and a trait for fearless leadership, Zhu rose quickly in the Red Turbans and formed a personal army along the Yangtze. He attacked and captured Nanjing in 1356, the first of many victories that followed. The city became his base of operations and, after a twelve-year campaign, Zhu proclaimed Nanjing to be the imperial capital of the Empire of the Great Ming, with himself as the Hongwu Emperor.

It was during this era that the Chinese developed and implemented both hand-held firearms and large cannons that fired cast-iron bombs. Thus equipped, Hongwu's army conquered the northern Yuan capital, which he renamed Beiping (the north is pacified), and the Mongols fled further north into Mongolia. He then conquered the remainder of China, along with Tibet and part of Korea.

The traditional centralized Tang-Song style of government utilized by the Mongols was continued by Hongwu. The country was stabilized and the dynasty survived for 276 years. Pride in the return of Han Chinese rule over a unified China for the first time since the Tang dynasty planted the seeds that would later ripen into nationalism.

Although limited in education, Hongwu was a quick learner and energetic ruler. He issued a flurry of edicts governing every aspect of government and civil life, and he defined the exact punishment for failure to abide by each directive.

Hongwu was a harsh disciplinarian. When he discovered a plot by his prime minister, he not only had the minister's head cut off, but he executed every member of the minister's family—no matter how remote—and more than 40,000 relatives were killed. Later purges increased the number of imperial executions to more than 100,000. Many more people were publically beaten and humiliated. Hongwu was sensitive to slight and fearful of rivals; he eventually executed almost all of his original supporters.

Ultimately, Hongwu eliminated the prime minister position and closed the central secretariat. Personally taking on the tasks of these two chancellors required him to review hundreds of communications and thousands of issues each week. With the head of central administration removed, Ming emperors came to increasingly rely on the household eunuchs of the Inner Court, who ultimately numbered 70,000.

Fiscally frugal, Hongwu kept taxes low, and paid nominal salaries to government officials—which encouraged corruption. At the same time, seeing little difference between official and personal expenses, his household expenditures grew enormously—as he came to employ a 75,000-member praetorian guard. The "Embroidered-uniform Guard" acted as an imperial police force and operated a prison for political offenders.

Peasants were registered and organized into groups of 110 households, which were further divided into subgroups of 10 families. Each year, a single rotating household had the responsibility to update the registers, collect taxes from the others, and arrange the public labor services required from the subgroup—such as maintenance of the Central Canal. In time, this system became as corrupt as the central administration.

In spite of an official animus toward merchants generally, trade continued to grow. Paper money was initially relied on; however, Hongwu began to print notes without properly backing them with coin. He forbade the minting of silver, and copper coins became scarce, resulting in widespread counterfeiting. As paper money became worthless, and with the great influx of silver from international trade, a two-metal system evolved in which copper was used for simple transactions, while silver bullion was relied on for more complex commercial deals. With the value of silver varying in different locales, currency traders were able to skim off profits, while other merchants and ordinary investors suffered.

Nonetheless, the status quo was somewhat maintained, as the Chinese people struggled to survive in a world that was becoming increasingly complicated—both economically and politically. The West was on the rise, and it would not be long before their ships arrived.

Upon his death in 1398, Hongwu was buried in a tomb near Nanjing, where his body remains to this day. Hongwu was ultimately succeeded by his son, Zhu Di, the Prince of Yan, who reigned as the Yongle emperor.

Yongle continued the despotic nature of Ming government, but appointed a chancellor over a grand secretariat, which included seven ministers, resulting in a more efficient and effective administration. Yongle gave extraordinary powers to the eunuch secret police and purged Confucian scholars from the government in Nanjing. In an attempt to control the scholars' power, he made a greater use of the imperial examination system.

Yongle had been originally assigned by his father, Hongwu to occupy Beiping, the capital of the Yuan dynasty. To secure better control over the northern border region—where the Mongols remained a threat—Yongle moved the capital from Nanjing to North China. One million workers were employed in building a magnificent new capital near Beiping, with a new palace and walls, which he named Beijing (northern capital), to differentiate it from Nanjing, the southern capital. The names of these two northern capitals are often combined and for much of the modern period, the name Peking prevailed in the West.

The Incredible Ming Navy

Ma He was a Muslim slave boy, who had been castrated to serve in Yongle's household. Renamed Zheng He, the boy was raised by Yongle, and he ultimately became the Grand Eunuch in charge of a special task force of eunuchs entrusted to carry out Yongle's favorite projects. One such project was the creation of a fleet of ships to engage in trade, survey the world, extend the limits of all under Heaven, and to increase the number of foreign rulers who acknowledged Chinese supremacy.

Commissioned as a fleet admiral, Zheng commanded some amazing voyages. The story is pretty spectacular, but before we set sail, we need a quick review of China's maritime history to better see where we are going and how we will get there.

There is evidence the early Neolithic Chinese were a seafaring, as well as agricultural people, and they probably reached Taiwan by sea as early as 4000 BCE. The Chinese were building large sailing ships that could tack close to the wind hundreds of years before the Common Era. There is good evidence these early Chinese ships crossed the Pacific Ocean and made landfall in Central and South America.

The Chinese were building ships with watertight bulkheads and steered by stern post rudders by the Second Century CE. One hundred years later they began to equip their ships with multiple masts and a redesigned square sail with fore-and-aft rigging, allowing ships to sail into the wind.

As early as the Han dynasty, the Chinese were regularly sailing to India. In reciprocity with the Arabs, trade routes along Southeast Asia and through the Indies were well established by the Tenth Century.

By 1000 CE, the Song had developed extensive celestial maps, which were useful in navigation, and they began to equip their sailing ships with navigational compasses. This invention allowed Chinese captains to navigate—even when they could not view the stars.

By the Thirteenth Century, the Chinese were dominating the Indian Ocean with standard ships that measured 100 feet long and 25 feet across. These merchant vessels could carry crews of 60 and cargos of 120 tons. There were even larger ships.

At the same time as China was conquering the northern part of Vietnam by land in the Seventh Century, two fleets were also dispatched

The Ming Dynasty, Its Mighty Navy, and the Great Wall

to invade the Ryukyu Islands near the Philippines, which are currently a matter of controversy. Apparently, the first invasion attempt was unsuccessful, and although the second was more successful, it was short-lived.

Once the Mongols had defeated China, Kublai tried to use the captured Song navy to launch oversea attacks, particularly against Japan. Using thousands of ships, his seaborne attack on Japan in 1274 failed due to bad weather and strong Japanese resistance. Much of his fleet was sunk and 13,000 troops lost their lives. A larger attack force in 1281 involving 140,000 troops was thwarted by a sudden typhoon, which the Japanese call a *kamikaze*, or "divine wind." More than 63,000 Chinese troops died in the second attempt.

Perhaps, because the caravan trade along the Silk Road (which the Mongols controlled) was so successful, the Yuan dynasty made less use of the captured Song navy for international trade. Even so, regular maritime commerce with Southeast Asia, Indonesia, India, and Sri Lanka was established. The trade was financed by investors and spread along the coast of China from Yangzhou to Guangzhou. The only reciprocal maritime commerce was by Arab traders.

At the beginning of the Fifteenth Century, Western nations, particularly Portugal and Spain, were reaching out with their sailing ships to find routes to the fabled China and the spices of the Orient. Sailing to the west in 1492, Spain found the way blocked by the Americas, and Portugal did not make it around Africa to India until 1498. While these feeble attempts were taking place in the West, let us now take a look at what China was already doing in the East.

Commencing in 1405, the Nanjing shipyards produced 2,000 ships, including nearly a hundred gigantic "treasure ships" measuring up to 440 feet in length, 186 feet across, and displacing 3,000 tons. The treasure ships were equipped with as many as nine 90-foot masts and red silk sails. They carried a complement of 500, and had as many as 60 cabins. The stern rudders are reported to have stood 36 feet high (the discovery of a stern post in 1957 near the Nanjing yard would have supported a 20-foot rudder).

In comparison, Columbus' largest ship, the *Santa Maria* was approximately 60 feet long, had a beam of 20 feet, a maximum displacement of 600 tons and carried a crew of 52. His other two ships, the *Nina* and *Pena* were tiny and carried only 18 men each. The modern U.S. destroyer is approximately 500 feet long, 66 feet in beam, and carries a crew of 300.

The first of seven voyages was launched in 1407 with 317 ships, including 62 treasure ships, carrying more than 27,000 naval and military personnel, and supply ships with grain and water. The first three trips were to India and intervening ports; the fourth went beyond to the Strait of Hormuz, and the last three reached the east coast of Africa, as far south as Kenya.

The primary purpose of the voyages was diplomacy and goodwill, with Zheng carrying ambassadors back and forth to China in the luxury staterooms. There was some trade and little fighting. No permanent settlements were erected and no metals were extracted. There was a side trip to Mecca, where Zheng's Muslim father had once made a pilgrimage to do his *Hajj*.

In May 1421, two months after the last voyage set sail, Yongle's palace in the Forbidden City in Beijing was struck by lightning and partially burned. There were a large number of deaths, including the emperor's favorite concubine. As Yongle lamented the loss, mandarin opponents of Zheng's voyages (who actually opposed *all* foreign trade and contact), used the disaster as a "heavenly warning" to advise against further exploration.

On a more practical level, construction of the fleets had leveled huge teak forests, and the drain on the treasury had been enormous. Combined with a deadly epidemic along the central coast and the precarious health of the emperor, world sea travel no longer seemed auspicious. Not only were future voyages prohibited, but there was a ban on all foreign travel.

Emperor Yongle died on August 12, 1424. He was succeeded by his son Zhu Gaozhi, who became the Hongxi Emperor. Hongxi had no interest in ocean adventures, and one of his first acts was to issue a decree stopping all voyages. The shipyards were closed, and the plans for the great ships were deliberately destroyed.

The Ming Dynasty, Its Mighty Navy, and the Great Wall

The Mercantile Invasion

Hongxi died after only one year and was succeeded by his son, Zhu Zhanji, who became the Xuande Emperor. China continued to retreat from the world, and most foreign trade was embargoed. The dynasty would continue for another two centuries, but it would never again look outward.

The Chinese hunkered down and began reconstruction and improvements on the system of Great Walls that had been built over the centuries along the northern border to protect against invasion. Continuing throughout the Ming dynasty, construction emphasized the use of parallel brick walls filled with rammed earth. Ultimately, the wall ran for 5,500 miles and had more than 10,000 watchtowers and beacon towers. It did not keep out the barbarians from the north, nor did the prohibition of ocean voyages keep out the barbarians from beyond the sea.

While China continued to be a strong and outwardly unified country, its government was slowly weakened by infighting and intrigue between the military, the bureaucracy (known as mandarins), and the eunuchs. The censorate reported directly to the emperor and had the power to impeach any official.

With time, the mandarins gained some control over the military, but the power of the eunuchs exceeded that of the bureaucracy. Supervision of the harem and inner court gave the eunuchs access and influence over the emperors, particularly when minors succeeded to the throne, as did eight of the eleven emperors in the last 200 years of Ming rule. Eunuchs commanded the secret police and the secretariat, and they managed the flow of information and correspondence. Several became dictators.

The government managed its vast land mass, population, and commerce through internal regulation and a complicated system of taxation on land and salt. The economy was, however, affected by events beyond the Chinese borders.

While China had destroyed its navy, looked inward and stagnated, other nations were looking outward. They were building larger and better ships, exploring the Americas and Africa, and international trade was expanding. Arabs continued to trade at Chinese ports, and the ships of the West began to call. With the flow of silver from the Americas to Spain and then on to other Western nations, the West had money to spend. Their power was growing, and they continued to desire what China produced.

The ships of the West flew the flags of their nations, and they claimed the lands and indigenous people they discovered for their monarchs. The vessels they sailed and the cargos they carried were, however, increasingly bought and paid for by trading companies organized for profit.

The Philippine islands, along the east side of the South China Sea, were claimed by Spain after Magellan landed there in 1521 and were quickly colonized. The Philippines became a transit and exchange point for the silver from the New World and the products of China.

Following the discovery voyages of Vasco de Gama, the Portuguese took a commanding lead in establishing maritime trade with India, China, and Japan. The Chinese treated the Portuguese with contempt; they initially allowed the Portuguese to anchor in the Macau harbor, but did not allow them to land. A permanent settlement was authorized in 1557 upon the payment of an annual rent of 41.6 pounds of silver. Trade outside of Macau was prohibited.

Underwritten by the massive amounts of gold and silver flowing from the New World, international trade came to be dominated by Western corporations. The Portuguese East India Company, the Dutch East India Company, and the British East India Company were all chartered by their governments for trade with India, China, and Japan. They received trade monopolies and had the power to deploy military force to defend their trade and to govern the land they conquered.

The Dutch colonized Taiwan in the early Seventeenth Century as a base for trade with China and Japan, and they built a fort in the area of Tainan in 1624.

In the West, the Spanish had quickly gained military and political power over much of Central and South America, and they enjoyed the bounty of the silver and gold produced by its colonies. Initially, Spain used the precious metals to purchase items manufactured or produced by

The Ming Dynasty, Its Mighty Navy, and the Great Wall

other nations, such as the English, French, and Dutch, which the Spanish re-exported to their colonies. In time, these countries sought to eliminate the middleman. Relying on state-authorized piracy, they began to seize the metals before they could arrive in Spain and to directly export their products to Spain's American colonies.

To avoid the pirates, Spain began to export silver directly from the west coast of Mexico to Manila in its Philippine colony, where it was primarily traded for silk—which had been shipped to Manila by Chinese merchants. The Pacific trade grew rapidly and more than two million pesos of silver were traded each year of the Seventeenth Century.

European wars of that period were often based on commercial competition involving the establishment and trade with colonies. In fighting these wars and making use of their growing industrial power, Western nations began to make use of the Chinese invention of gunpowder to create weapons that could be used to enforce and protect corporate trading. Human slavery figured in the calculus of the supply and demand of sugar and rum. The absence of a conscience factor in the equation posed an increasing danger to anyone or anything that stood in the way of corporate profit.

By the Seventeenth Century, the Ming dynasty of China was producing substantial amounts of silk and cotton cloth, tea, porcelain, and other exotic items, such as laquerwork and silk paintings, for export. There was a brisk international trade between Chinese merchants and outsiders, who paid for their purchases in silver, rivers of which flowed into China each year. With the privatization of the salt and iron monopolies, low taxes, and an import economy, merchants began to gain power, relative to that of the government.

The Chinese economy's growing dependence on foreign trade made it susceptible to external problems. A financial depression hit the West in 1620, and the Little Ice Age of 1650 in Europe had a ripple effect in China—which experienced an economic downturn. As the power of the government continued to weaken, rural banditry began to increase, rebellions sprang up, and the security of the nation collapsed.

Descended from the Jurchen tribes that formed the earlier Jin empire, the Manchu came to power in the area of Manchuria. We may recall the Southern Song made an alliance with the Mongols allowing them to defeat the Jurchens. Once again, the Chinese had reason to regret that decision, as the Manchu avenged it.

The first major raid by the Manchu in 1629 was repulsed. Continuing invasions forced the Ming government to deploy its military to protect its northern border, and internal rebellions were not repressed. By this point, the government was bankrupt, and it no longer controlled its own territory. Chinese rebel forces seized Beijing in 1644, and the emperor committed suicide.

The Manchu arrived just in time to "save" the Ming dynasty and defeat the rebels in Beijing. When the Manchu occupied the city, the Ming government retreated south to Nanjing. The invasion pushed south taking Yangzhou at the intersection of the Yangtze river and Grand Canal. When Guangzhou fell, the last Ming emperor escaped to Burma, where he was later captured and executed.

Ming resistance was continued by Zheng Chenggong, or Koxinga, who was either a pirate, armed trader, or patriot, depending on who tells the story. Having earlier formed an alliance with the Dutch, Zheng commanded a large naval force, which he used to sail up the Yangtze and threaten the Manchu in Nanjing. He was driven away and retreated with his forces to Taiwan, where the Dutch surrendered to him in 1661. He established the "Ming Eastern Capital;" his descendants formed a Chinese government in exile and claimed leadership of the overseas Chinese.

In 1670, Chenggong's son, Zheng Jing, whom the English called the "King of Tywan" concluded a trade agreement allowing England a land base on Taiwan. The English were to later use their foothold on Taiwan to open up trade with mainland China.

After the Manchu invaded Taiwan in 1683, Zheng surrendered and Taiwan was incorporated into the Manchu Qing dynasty.

There was a new dynasty ruling China. Its emperor was not Chinese, but it was to be the last Chinese dynasty.

The Manchurian Qing Dynasty

The Manchu invasion of China was commanded by Dorgon, who was acting as regent for his five-year-old nephew, the Shunzhi Emperor of the Manchu Qing dynasty. Following the capture of Beijing in 1644, the boy was installed as the "Son of Heaven," becoming the emperor of China.

Dorgon sought to reassure the Chinese people by retaining many of the Ming officials and the civil service examination system. He declared the empire to be "a single whole," and there was to be no difference between the Manchu and Han Chinese.

The war of conquest for China by the Manchu was fought with gunpowder weapons by both sides. Hundreds of cannons were manufactured, some weighing more than three tons and firing 22-pound cannonballs. Coordinated bombardments were used in many assaults on walled cities, and muskets were in common use.

As the remainder of the country was conquered, the main requirement imposed on the Han Chinese was for them to shave their foreheads and grow a Manchu-style queue (pigtail) as a sign of submission.

Dorgon died in 1650, and factional infighting failed to provide strong leadership for the young emperor, Shunzhi, who came under the influence of the surviving Ming ministers and a German Jesuit missionary. The emperor welcomed Han Chinese mandarins into his government, reestablished the Secretariat and increased the power of the Chinese eunuchs—who occupied key financial and political posts. Shunzhi learned the Chinese language and developed an appreciation of Chinese art and literature.

Following Shunzhi's sudden death in 1661 at the age of 22, his seven-year-old son succeeded him and became Emperor Kangxi. The boy's power was exercised by four Manchu regents, who eliminated the Secretariat in an attempt to restrict the power acquired by the mandarins and eunuchs. When Kangxi assumed personal power in 1669, he lifted some of these restrictions and reestablished the Secretariat and its attendant authority.

The entire area of China was not completely subdued until 1683, with the capture of Taiwan; however, the Qing dynasty was already becoming accepted on the mainland. Chinese scholars, who at first had refused to serve the Qing, were invited to take a special examination and to work with the new dynasty. One of the first assignments was to complete a comprehensive history of the Ming dynasty. The scholars were also commissioned to prepare a massive encyclopedia and a compilation of every historical and philosophical work ever written in the Chinese language. When completed, the anthology comprised 36,000 volumes and was too large to print.

Kangxi worked hard to become a *Chinese* ruler, and he largely overcame Chinese resistance to the Qing dynasty during his 61-year reign. He generally continued neo-Confucian principles and sought the moral approval of his subjects. Kangxi is considered to have been one of the most outstanding Chinese emperors. His reign was mostly a time of peace, prosperity, and expansion as he brought together all of China, the Russian Far East, Outer and Inner Mongolia, Tibet, and Taiwan.

Once the Zheng regime had been defeated on Taiwan and Kanxi no longer feared a waterborne invasion in the south, he issued a decree allowing foreign trade:

> Now the whole country is unified, everywhere there is peace and quiet. Manchu-Han relations are fully integrated so I command you to go abroad and trade to show the populous and affluent nature of our rule. By imperial decree I open the seas to trade.

Foreign traders received consent to enter China in 1685. The next year Kangxi established the Ocean Trading House in Canton (modern

The Manchurian Qing Dynasty

Guangzhou) as a trading monopoly through which to funnel all foreign trade in and out of China. Guangzhou was adjacent to the Portuguese enclave at Macau.

In 1745, Chinese merchants became responsible for all arriving ships, officers, and crew, and the payment of all taxes. A group of Guangzhou merchant families known as the Cohong (or Hong) were appointed to serve as the intermediary between the government and foreign traders. They were responsible for harbor operations, and they received a monopoly to buy and sell goods from and to foreigners, and to collect all taxes on behalf of the government. In 1757, all foreign trade, except for Russia, was banned from other Chinese ports. More severe restrictions were issued after an English trader attempted to complain about trade matters.

At the end of the Eighteenth Century, China was exporting millions of pieces of "Chinaware" and countless bolts of silk each year, and thousands of Chinese worked at hundreds of imperial kilns and looms. In fact, while China represented a potential market as large as all of Europe and the Americas combined, the West produced little China desired. China was self-sufficient in most of its needs.

In 1792, England dispatched Lord Macartney as an ambassador to Beijing, to negotiate a trading treaty. The enormous cost of the trip was underwritten by the East India Company. As gifts, the Lord brought examples of English manufacturing, including Wedgewood pottery, a planetarium, and two howitzers (all of which the Chinese already possessed in abundance). The emperor graciously accepted the gifts, but refused to allow Macartney to remain in Beijing. The emperor of "all under Heaven" was superior to all other rulers and did not make treaties with them.

In his written response to the King of England, the emperor said: "As your Ambassador can see for himself, we possess all things. I set no value on objects strange or ingenious and have no use for your country's manufactures."

The Qing encouraged the creation of wealth and generally supported trade. The economy was a combination of imperial-owned industries (such as porcelain and silk manufacturing, tea, salt, and matches) and independent, home-based producers. Indeed, the productivity and low cost of the handicrafts produced in the countryside was one reason why urban workshops could not compete, and why mechanized industry did not gain a greater foothold in China.

The Qing shared the Ming's lack of interest in maritime trade. Thus, while England and other Western countries were rapidly expanding the power of their navies to support their commercial activity, the Qing were acting to secure the marginal benefits of controlling the land trade routes through Central Asia.

The Qing's rule over China was to last for 268 years, until 1912. During much of that time, the primary invasions it had to cope with were those launched by Western corporations to enrich themselves at China's expense.

Occupying a land mass of 3,700,000 square miles with natural borders, China had maintained a continuity of central government, by and large, for four thousand years. There was little beyond those borders that the Chinese wanted or needed. In contrast to England, which had been terrorizing other nations for centuries, China was mostly peaceful and wanted to be left alone. The corporate powers of the Western maritime nations wanted China as a vast market for their products—their salesmen had a foot in the door, and they were not to be denied entry.

In addition to learning the marvelous history of the Chinese culture, as we have thus far, experiencing what happened to that culture as a result of Western greed and exploitation will help us understand what is taking place in China today.

THE CORPORATE-INDUSTRIAL COLONIZATION OF CHINA

The English were to repay the Chinese for their humiliation of Lord Macartney many times over during the following century. In his report, Macartney noted that the trade of opium and cotton from India had become "necessities" in China. Observing the poor strength of the Chinese armaments, he believed the forts of Guangzhou could be leveled with "half a dozen broadsides" and that the British Navy could easily destroy Chinese costal shipping. He mused about whether the Qing dynasty could survive having its power broken by the English Navy: "She may drift sometime as a wreck, and will then be dashed to pieces on the shore; but she can never be rebuilt on the same bottom." He concluded the Chinese had become "semi-barbarians," whose trade objections could be swept aside and who could be colonized—as the Western powers were doing around the world.

English woolens and metal goods were the only items the British East India Company offered that the Chinese were willing to accept in trade for tea. By the middle of the Eighteenth Century, the balance of trade favored the Chinese and the difference had to be paid in silver. As the English tea addiction grew (nine million pounds imported in 1770), so did the balance of payment deficit. To offset silver payments for tea, the English began to ship more opium to China, along with raw cotton from India. Although the sale of opium was illegal in England, the East India Company saw nothing wrong with selling it in China in order to balance its books. The fact that opium was also prohibited in China was of no concern to the corporation.

The East India Company had the monopoly for opium production in Bengal and was exporting 240 tons of opium per year to China as early as 1796. The trade accounts moved out of the red. By 1820, silver was flowing out of China at a rate of nearly 11,000,000 ounces a year.

Even so, the East India Company lost its monopoly over China trade in 1834. Its agent in Guangzhou was replaced by a British official assigned to oversee all English traders at the port. He refused to deal with the Hong shipping families and demanded to deal directly with Qing officials as an equal. The dynasty struggled to arrive at a policy to respond to English demands and to control the opium trade, which was destroying Chinese lives and disrupting the economy by reversing the flow of silver.

Since the English had prevailed in the Napoleonic Wars and had become the supreme naval power in the world, the Chinese feared that England's steam-powered gunboats could overpower any resistance they might be able to offer. Nonetheless, the Chinese concluded there was no real choice but to take action to stop the drug trade.

An incorruptible superintendent was dispatched to Guangzhou with instructions to clean up the situation. He quickly arrested the most notorious Chinese drug dealers and locked up the foreign importers in their warehouses, until they agreed to surrender their stock of 980 tons of opium. The importers were forced to sign bonds—upon penalty of death—promising they would never again import opium, and their drugs were destroyed. The English considered the Chinese law enforcement action to be an act of war.

The English were not alone in the opium trade, with Yankee entrepreneurs trading ginseng grown in New York and opium produced in Turkey for tea and other Chinese products. Among those growing rich in the drug business was Warren Delano, the maternal grandfather of U.S. President Franklin Delano Roosevelt. Delano, among those caught up by Chinese law enforcement, wrote home protesting that the opium trade had been "fair, honorable, and legitimate."

William Napier, the English Superintendent of Trade in China, wrote about how easy it would be to "raise a revolution and cause them

The Corporate-Industrial Colonization Of China

to open their ports to the trading world. I should like to be the medium of such a change."

An expeditionary force was sent from India and, as predicted by Lord Macartney, it quickly destroyed all Chinese resistance. Guangzhou officials were forced to pay $6 million to avoid an attack. The expeditionary force quickly secured the Chinese coast, after a number of one-sided assaults on port cities. After Shanghai was occupied and gunboats began to move up the Yangtze river toward Nanjing, the Qing capitulated and signed the Treaty of Nanjing.

The English received all they demanded. Four more ports, in addition to Guangzhou and including Shanghai, were opened to English trade, and Xianggang (Hong Kong) was ceded to England. As a final insult, China was forced to pay $21 million for the destroyed opium and England's war expenses.

Given the unequal bargaining power of the parties, the agreement would be considered a *nudum pactum* (naked promise), and would be unenforceable under English contract law for the lack of an adequate consideration. The treaty was the be the first of many such "agreements" during the Nineteenth Century that stole the land, sovereignty, and dignity of China.

The subsequent Treaty of Bogue allowed the exemption of foreigners from the jurisdiction of Chinese courts (extraterritoriality), which could be extended to all other nations. Import tariffs were frozen at five percent. The United States' first treaty with China was thusly accorded the same benefits as the English. When France obtained imperial toleration of Roman Catholics in China, religious forbearance was extended to all other Christians.

The English, who had been trading from Hong Kong, were promised entry into Guangzhou by 1849; however the Chinese tried to resist further foreign intrusion and delayed access. A change of emperor in 1850 and the Crimean War of 1854 put off an English response. An incident—in which the Chinese boarded a small boat (which claimed English registration) to arrest pirates—was considered an insult to the English flag, and another expeditionary force was sent to China.

Once again, the English quickly took Guangzhou and steamed up the coast, defeating the Dagu forts. The Qing capitulated and signed the Treaty of Tianjin, which opened ten more treaty ports and allowed Christian missionaries free access to the interior. The opium trade was legalized, and a British ambassador was allowed to establish an embassy in Beijing. Similar treaties were quickly signed by Russia, France, and the United States; however, their representatives were blocked in 1859, when they attempted to travel to Beijing to ratify the treaties.

An English-led allied force returned the next year, burned the Summer Palace and entered Beijing. Another one-sided treaty opened up Tianjin to trade, ceded the Kowloon peninsula adjacent to Hong Kong to England, and once again required China to pay for the war. One month later, Russia forced China to cede territory allowing the establishment of a naval base at Vladivostok.

Historians have advanced many different reasons for China's failure to resist the Western corporate-industrial invasion, many of which are quite complicated. The simplest answer may be that for almost 4,000 years the Chinese had lived by a philosophy based upon moral principles derived from the natural universe, rather than divine revelation.

The Chinese were content with what they had and desired nothing from the West but to be left alone. Their culture had continued uninterrupted, as invading forces had come and gone, and other great empires had risen and fallen. The rest of the world was struggling to get to China, but China was already there.

For many good reasons, the Chinese believed in the superiority of their system. They were content to live within and to defend their borders, as necessary, and did not believe their security was enhanced by the subjugation of others.

Perhaps they were wrong, but we can only imagine how much different the world would be today if the tiny ships of Columbus and Vasco de Gama had been confronted with the mighty Chinese dreadnoughts armed with cannons and rockets, as the Western explorers attempted to venture

The Corporate-Industrial Colonization Of China

into uncharted waters. Most likely, we would all be speaking Chinese, instead of wondering whether our children should be studying it.

As the Nineteenth Century came to a close, a much-reduced China was facing extraordinary difficulties in coping with the military and economic burdens that had been placed on its people and their emperor. It was to be more than his dynasty could endure, and it was to put the Chinese people to the most severe test in their 4,000-year history.

A Troubling Matter of Diplomacy

Having defeated all opponents, England ruled the oceans around the world in the opening days of the Twentieth Century. Two new challengers were, however, sailing into the seas of China.

The Japanese had defeated China in the Sino-Japanese War of 1894, obtaining most-favored nation treatment and forcing the cession of Taiwan and the Liaodong Peninsula (which juts southwest out of China above its border with Korea) in settlement. Japan seized the Ruyukyu archipelago, including Okinawa, from China in 1879, and defeated Russia in the Russo-Japanese War in 1905.

The United States had forced the opening of Japan to outside trade in 1853, purchased Alaska in 1867, annexed Hawaii in 1898, and, in the same year, defeated Spain in the Spanish American War—thereby seizing the Philippines as a U.S. colony in the South China Sea.

The treaty executed between America and China in 1844 introduced the United States as a player on the Chinese stage. Promising "Peace, Amity, and Commerce," the treaty extended extraterritoriality protection to Americans and most-favored nation status equivalent to that earlier obtained by England and other powers. One significant difference was an agreement that the opium trade was illegal, and the United States agreed to surrender offenders to China. Most importantly for the discussion which follows was the introductory clause which stated:

> There shall be a perfect, permanent, universal peace, and a sincere and cordial amity, between the United States of America on the one part,

and the Ta Tsing [Qing] Empire on the other part, and between their people respectively, without exception of persons or places.

Although the United States was to later participate in the Eight Nation Alliance during the Boxer Rebellion in 1900, the relationship between the United States and China was never as adversarial as China experienced with other Western countries.

The Treaty opened the interior of China to American missionary activity, and the churches of the United States quickly responded. By 1900, more than 1,000 Christian missionaries and their families were living and spreading the gospel of Christianity in China. The missionaries established schools and hospitals and, given the difficulty of language, worked to make life easier for the Chinese people and to convert them from the Buddhist and Confucian beliefs they practiced.

From all of this, it appeared the United States had good intentions to ensure the "perfect, permanent, universal peace" it had promised. Indeed, during World War II, the United States participated mightily in the defense of China. Something happened, however, in the early years of the Twentieth Century, which may have contributed to the harm later suffered by the Chinese people during that war. The United States, by its involvement in that earlier incident, may share some responsibility for what occurred. These events are troubling and need to be discussed, if there is to be a full understanding of the essential history of China.

The incident did not involve China directly, but concerned Korea, which had been a tributary of China for centuries. Moreover, it reflected a "tilt" by the United States toward Japan and away from its friendship with China.

In 1882, the United States signed a Treaty of Peace, Amity, Commerce, and Navigation with Korea. The treaty promised mutual friendship, but in addition, *each side pledged to provide mutual assistance in case of attack.*

China ceded the Liaodong Peninsula to Japan following its defeat in the Sino-Japanese War, but Japan was quickly forced to withdraw from the peninsula by the Triple Intervention of Russia, Germany, and France.

A Troubling Matter of Diplomacy

Russia occupied part of the Peninsula and constructed Port Arthur as a warm-water port.

While this occupation by Russia was one of the causes of the Russo-Japanese War, another was a dispute over which nation had spheres of influence over Korea and Manchuria. The war began with a surprise Japanese attack on Port Arthur, and major battles were fought along the Yulu River, which divides China (Manchuria) and Korea.

Japan had commenced its colonization of Korea by forcing it to sign a treaty in 1876, ending Korea's tributary relationship with China and opening its ports to Japanese trade.

In August 1900, a concerned Korean Emperor Gojong was reassured by U.S. Minister Horace Allen "that the United States would indeed exercise good offices in accord with the treaty of 1882 should the occasion arise." Good offices is a diplomatic term providing third-party mediation of a dispute.

Theodore Roosevelt became president of the United States in 1901, and his attitude toward Japan and its consequences are pertinent. Before becoming president, Theodore Roosevelt wrote, "I should like to see Japan have Korea. She will be a check upon Russia, and she deserves it for what she has done." Once he was president, Roosevelt praised Japan's victory over Russia, "I was thoroughly well pleased with the Japanese victory, for Japan is playing our game."

On February 23, 1904, Korea was forced to sign a treaty which established Japan's protectorate over Korea. Emperor Gojong requested assistance from the United States. On April 14, 1904, Minister Allen wrote to the Secretary of State:

> The Emperor confidently expects that America will do something for him at the close of this war, or when opportunity offers, to retain for him as much of his independence as is possible . . . . I am obliged to assure His Majesty that the condition of Korea is borne in mind by the United States Government, who will use their good offices when occasion occurs.

Shortly thereafter the Japanese burned the Emperor's palace, and Minister Allen refused the Emperor's request for political asylum.

At about the same time, Roosevelt was impressed with the arrival of Japan's special envoy, Baron Kaneko, who had received a law degree from Harvard. It was Kaneko's mission to obtain U.S. assistance in ending the war with Russia and to obtain a three-party agreement for England, the United States, and Japan to have an "open-door" into China.

During a number of conversations, Roosevelt made it clear he envisioned a strong role for Japan in the Orient, as long as Japan had no designs on the Philippines. The only documentation of the off-the-record talks is provided by Kaneko's memorandum, which paraphrased Roosevelt:

> Japan is the only nation in Asia that understands the principles and methods of Western civilization. She has proved that she can assimilate Western civilization, yet not break up her own heritage. All the Asiatic nations are now faced with the urgent necessity of adjusting themselves to the present age. Japan should be their natural leader in that process, and their protector during the transition stage, much as the United States assumed the leadership of the American continent many years ago, and by means of the Monroe Doctrine, preserved the Latin American nations from European interference, while they were maturing their independence.... The future policy of Japan towards Asiatic countries should be similar to that of the United States towards their neighbors on the American continent. A "Japanese Monroe Doctrine" in Asia will remove the temptation to European encroachment, and Japan will be recognized as the leader of the Asiatic nations, and her power will form the shield behind which they can reorganize their national systems.

In February 1905, future South Korean president Syngman Rhee arrived in Washington, DC on behalf of Emperor Gojong to plead with the United States to honor its treaty obligation. He was reassured by Secretary of State John Hay: "I will do everything I can to fulfill our treaty obligations, either personally, or representing the United States government, whenever the opportunity presents itself."

Hay's promise was not kept, and in 1907, Korea was forced to sign another treaty ceding administrative control of the country to Japan. The same year, Emperor Gojong sent representatives to the Second Peace Conference at The Hague attempting to bring Korea's problems to world attention. Although the Japanese blocked their attendance, the Koreans spoke to the gathered news media: "The United States does not realize what Japan's policy in the Far East is and what it portends for the American People."

All of this was to no avail, as Japan forced Korea to sign yet another treaty in 1910, which totally annexed Korea to Japan. Emperor Gojong was forced to abdicate, and he was likely poisoned to death by the Japanese in 1919, the same year Theodore Roosevelt died.

Korea did not regain its independence until the end of World War II.

What does all of this mean? We know Japan used the concept of a Greater East Asia Co-Prosperity Sphere to justify its invasions of Manchuria, China, and other Asian countries. Would Japan have acted so aggressively without having been encouraged to promulgate an Asian Monroe Doctrine? Possibly. If, however, the United States had fulfilled the "good offices" of its treaty with Korea, Japan may have been prevented from annexing Korea. Moreover, had the United States assertively allied itself with England and the other Western nations, Japan may have been deterred from invading Manchuria and China. Indeed, had the Western democracies united and acted together in such a forthright manner against all fascist aggression, World War II might have been avoided altogether.

We will never know what might have been, but we do know what did in fact happen—or we are about to learn—and it is time to raise the curtain on another act in the drama of China's history.

Part Two: The Communist Dynasty

Death Throes of an Empire

By the close of the Nineteenth Century, the Qing dynasty was no longer governing China. Internal order began to break down, resulting in a rise in rebellions and the organization of local self-defense forces or militias by local gentry to keep the peace. In addition to a failing economy, the root cause of the two largest political rebellions of the period had religious undertones.

China attempted to strengthen its internal and external integrity, but found itself incapable of containing the onslaught of Western incursions and defending itself in a war against Japan.

The Taiping Rebellion (1851-1864)

After the Qing dynasty resumed the civil service examination system, a 22-year-old teacher, who was in Guangzhou to take the 1836 examination, was handed some Christian tracts by a missionary. After failing the examination, the student became ill and had a dream in which an old man handed him a sword and a younger man fought at his side against demons. After failing the examination three more times, he reread the Christian tracts and imagined they were the answer to his vision. The old man was the Christian God, the younger man was Jesus Christ and he, Hong Xiuquan, was God's Chinese son. The sword was to root out idolatry.

Hong shared his revelation and converted one cousin as a disciple. As "no man is a prophet in his own village," Hong took his ministry to Guangzhou, where he soon attracted 2,000 God Worshippers. Two of his disciples experienced their own visions in which one was Jesus and the other was God's spokesman. United by prophetic zeal, they set out to destroy Buddhist and Confucian shrines.

Considered rebels, they were attacked by government soldiers and the gentry militia—whereupon Hong proclaimed himself to be the Heavenly King of the Heavenly Kingdom of Great Peace. Christian missionaries provided initial support, but they soon proclaimed Hong to be a blasphemer, rather than a prophet.

Hong and his main disciples took multiple concubines and lived lives of luxury. Animal sacrifices were offered in the Taiping temples, and Hong was referred to as "Our Lord."

Moving to unseat the foreign Qing dynasty as alien usurpers, Hong created a military organization and began a northward march, gathering 1,000,000 followers. He captured Nanjing, which he designated as his capital. The crusade continued northward and almost captured Beijing, before being turned back. Opposed by gentry militia and government troops, the civil war raged across more than half of China for seven years, during which time 600 walled cities changed hands and as many as 30 million people died.

In 1860, French, American, and British troops joined with Qing forces to subdue the rebellion, fielding a force known as the Ever Victorious Army. The army was financed by Shanghai businessmen and led by an American, Frederick Townsend Ward, who had become a Chinese citizen and married a Chinese wife. He was later killed in a battle against the Taiping rebels.

When Nanjing was recaptured in 1864, Hong either committed suicide or died of supernatural causes. While unsuccessful, the rebellion was the first to express a nationalist cause against the foreign Qing dynasty.

Following the rebellion, the Chinese army was culturally and religiously divided into Manchu, Han Chinese, Muslim, and Mongol armies, which were further deployed into independent regional commands. These local units would in the future become the armies of warlords.

The Taiping Rebellion was the most destructive war of the Nineteenth Century and the bloodiest civil war in history.

Death Throes of an Empire

Self Strengthening Movement (1861-1895)

One positive contribution of the missionary movement and its need to translate Christian religious materials into Chinese was the development of a standardized written and spoken language. For most of its existence, the Empire of China had been managed by mandarins, trained and tested in the Confucian classics. They spoke and wrote in a highly refined medium, which used some 4,000 written characters. Many characters, representing objects or abstract ideas and individual syllables, were beyond the understanding of most Chinese people. General literacy, to the limited extent it existed, was based on a much smaller group of written characters and a simpler speech. Ordinary people could not read the classics or imperial documents.

The Chinese written language was more than 3,000 years old, and its system of written characters was universal. It could be used to represent different languages, such as Korean and Japanese, and different dialects of the Chinese spoken language. Indeed, residents of one village might have trouble understanding people in a neighboring village, but each could read the written words of the other.

The interpretation of Chinese and the transliteration of the language into the alphabetic, sound-based, Roman lettering of Western languages was extremely difficult. Not only must the characters, which have multiple meanings depending upon the context, be interpreted, but different Chinese dialects produce different transliterations.

As a part of its effort to increase literacy, modernize its society and make use of Western knowledge and technology, an effort was made to produce a simpler written language using fewer characters and requiring fewer brushstrokes. Incorporating new grammatical structures and foreign loan-words, the language was adapted; yet it retained its uniquely Chinese character.

In the mid-Nineteenth Century, several writers began to advocate making use of Western techniques and technology to build weapons and ships to defend China. They urged the expansion of translation training and the study of Western languages, science, and mathematics, in addition to the Chinese classics. In essence, Confucian philosophy and ethics were to be supplemented by Western methods in an effort to strengthen China's ability to resist aggression. The first step was to establish a number of foreign language schools.

Recognizing that China did not have the industrial capacity to manufacture modern weapons, efforts were made to buy manufacturing technology and machines. First limited to the manufacture of small arms, modest ship building and naval school programs followed.

A domestic steamship line was licensed to compete with foreign shipping, and coal mining—using advanced Western technology—was initiated to fuel the ships. A national telegraph system was created. All of these efforts were delayed and obstructed by the mandarin bureaucratic scholars.

Some small ships were built in China, but two battleships were purchased from Germany, as well as large cruisers from England. Funds earmarked for additional naval development were shifted to the construction of the Empress Dowager's summer palace (which was later burned by the Allied army during the Boxer Rebellion).

Germany also assisted in fortifying Port Arthur, on the Liaodong Peninsula, and the Weihaiwei naval base, on the Shandong Peninsula, with Krupp artillery. These two peninsulas jut out toward each other from the Chinese mainland, encompassing the Bohai Sea.

Foreign advisors were hired to train the Chinese military in the operation of the purchased ships and weapons. Critically, however, little formal military education was provided on the tactics and strategies of modern warfare that had been developed in the West. As with its rapid industrialization and military modernization, Japan had learned these lessons; thus, it had the advantage in its war with China.

The Sino-Japanese War (1894-1895)

Although an independent nation with its own monarchy, Korea had paid tribute to China for hundreds of years. In 1876, Japan forced Korea to open its ports to trade and gained other rights for Japanese residents. In

Death Throes of an Empire

the Convention of Tientsin of 1885, Japan and China agreed to restrict sending troops to Korea.

When the Korean king requested assistance in 1894 to quell a rebellion, the Chinese sent 2,800 troops. The Japanese claimed they were not informed, as required by the 1885 treaty, and sent their own force of 8,000. The rebellion was quickly suppressed, and Japanese troops arrived just as the Chinese force was departing. Japan nonetheless occupied the royal palace and held the Korean king hostage. The government was taken over by pro-Japanese sympathizers, who requested the Japanese army to expel the Chinese forces.

Though violent, the resulting war was so brief as to limit the number of words needed to describe it. The Chinese did not have enough guns for its soldiers or ammunition for its guns, and they were quickly thrown out of Korea.

In the battle of the Yalu River, a fleet of Chinese warships, that had just escorted a supply convey, was confronted by a Japanese fleet. Although the Chinese fleet was larger and included battleships with bigger guns, it was commanded by an old army cavalry general who ordered an advance on the Japanese force with his ships spread out in a line like a cavalry charge. The better trained and agile Japanese fleet decimated it.

The remaining Chinese fleet was later found to be hiding under the German-supplied shore guns of the Weihaiwei naval base on the Shandong Peninsula. Japanese marines captured the high ground and turned the German shore guns on the Chinese fleet, sinking one battleship and four cruisers. The remainder surrendered, and the Chinese no longer had a navy. The Japanese occupied the Shandong Peninsula and threatened the heart of China.

The war ended on April 17, 1895 and a treaty ceded Taiwan and the Liaodong Peninsula, with Port Arthur, to Japan. An alliance of Russia, France, and Germany quickly forced Japan to surrender its treaty rights to the Liaodong Peninsula, and Port Arthur was occupied by Russia as a warm-water port on the Pacific. Japan retained Taiwan.

Once again, China was forced to pay for the costs of the lost war, amounting to a total of 276,000,000 troy ounces of silver. This would amount to more than $6 billion at the present price of silver.

The Boxer Rebellion (1898-1900)

In the final days of the Nineteenth Century, it appeared China was being divided into separate colonies by the Western powers, and the Qing dynasty was powerless to stop it. The Western commercial and religious colonization of China caused widespread economic disruptions and discontent.

Confronted with famine, severe drought, and floods, and resentful of Christian missionary activity, many Chinese began to seek answers in secret societies. One was the Righteous and Harmonious Fists, who were known as the Boxers. They were a group of athletic young men who believed that through prayer, diet, and martial arts training they could fly and become invulnerable.

The Boxers hated foreign influence and missionaries, and generally supported the government. In 1898, a group of Boxers attacked a Catholic church, which had been converted from a Jade Emperor temple. Their battle cry was, "Support the Qing, destroy the foreigners."

Encouraged by the Empress Dowager Cixi and Manchu conservatives, the movement quickly spread into and around the Beijing area. Churches were burned, and hundreds of Christian missionaries and their families were killed, along with thousands of Chinese Christians.

At this stage of Western occupation, a Legation Section had been established in Beijing, and the diplomats' request to allow their own military to protect them against the Boxers was granted. A small international force of 435 soldiers quickly arrived. Following a number of provocative incidents by both sides, a larger foreign relief force was dispatched from Tianjin—without permission of the imperial government. A pro-Boxer faction of the Chinese government came to power and ordered imperial troops to attack the approaching relief force. The relief force was cut off and had to be rescued by a third international force.

Realizing the Boxers had widespread domestic support, Empress Dowager Cixi declared war on all foreign powers. The Foreign Legation, along with a Catholic Cathedral, was under siege for 55 days by thousands of Chinese soldiers and Boxer rebels.

Death Throes of an Empire

A more moderate Manchu faction began to prevail and managed to prevent a direct assault on the Legation. The siege was called off and steps were taken to suppress the Boxers. An armistice was declared and mostly prevailed until the Eight-Nation Alliance arrived in Beijing in August.

The United States contributed 5,000 troops to the Alliance, a unilateral decision by President William McKinley—without a declaration of war. This was the first use of such unitary presidential power to defeat indigenous social and religious movements, but as events in the following century in countries such as Panama, Afghanistan, Somalia, Iraq, and Yemen, repeatedly demonstrated, it was not the last.

A total of 55,000 foreign troops were ultimately involved in the Boxer Rebellion, with 20,000 making up the main attack force. It was horribly hot, and the invasion was marred by extreme violence, rape, and pillaging.

Beijing was occupied for the next year and suffered what has been called an "orgy of looting." The plunder from one American diplomat alone required several railroad cars to haul away. As a condition of withdrawing the international troops, the Allies demanded the execution of ten government officials and required others to either commit suicide or be banished. Once again, China had to pay for the war in an amount equal to almost $10 billion today.

Although the Allies prevailed in the end, there were several times during the rebellion in which it appeared the Chinese might win. The ability of the Chinese to acquit themselves against the Western powers would be acclaimed in the future by Mao Zedong as a heroic resistance against foreign capitalists.

One final consequence of the Qing's defeat in the Boxer Rebellion was the occupation of Manchuria by Russia. Any hope of maintaining China as an empire, indeed even as a nation, was dimming.

In spite of China's suffering as a result of Western colonization, both the population and the economy had expanded. The trading ports had improved street lighting and water systems. A business class was developed, and Chambers of Commerce were established.

Young men went abroad to study—mostly to Japan—where they learned about the leading role the military could take in transforming a nation. When they returned home to China, many of them joined the New Army units, which became hotbeds of nationalism.

More newspapers and magazines printed in the vernacular allowed ordinary people to read and to form opinions about matters such as nationalism and self-government. Labor unions were being organized in some of the larger cities, particularly Shanghai. There were street protests and boycotts—notably in 1905—against restrictions on Chinese immigration into the United States.

China had learned over the years to roll with the punches from the Western nations. Being defeated by Japan—a former tributary—was, however, a body blow, not only from a military standpoint, but from a cultural one as well. There was a real question whether the mantle of heaven had been lifted from the Qing dynasty.

Nationalism and the Republican Revolution

Even though the Empress Dowager Cixi exercised the power of the Qing dynasty during Boxer Rebellion, the throne was actually occupied by her nephew. Following the death of his father when he was four years old, Emperor Guangxu had been adopted by his aunt, and she became his regent.

Cixi refused to step aside when Guangxu came of age to govern independently in 1887, and he began his rule under her close supervision. Cixi retired after her niece married the emperor in 1889, but she kept Guangxu on a tight rein.

An avid reader, Guangxu came under the influence of progressive writers, who sought to impose social change from the top down. During a 100-day period starting in June 1898, Guangxu issued 40 reform decrees to build a modern education system; update the examination system; increase the speed of industrialization; apply capitalistic principles; and, most importantly perhaps, change the government into a more democratic constitutional monarchy.

Cixi responded with a military *coup d'état*. The 27-year-old emperor was isolated within Beijing's Forbidden City, where he would remain until his death—by arsenic poisoning at her hand in 1908. Six of his advisors were immediately executed, depriving the liberalization movement of its leadership and causing others to flee or remain silent.

Nothing immediately came of Guangxu's attempt to impose a constitutional monarchy, but the seeds of freedom had been planted. It took a decade for them to sprout. Some who tended the garden hoped for a parliamentary monarchy, as in Japan. Others wanted a representative democracy, as had flourished throughout the Americas and much of Europe in the last century. Yet others wanted Marxism, which was soon to sprout in Russia. All were motivated by a sense of nationalism, their great resentment of foreign colonization, and the failure of the foreign dynasty that ruled China to do anything about it.

Bending to internal pressure, the Empress Dowager allowed some progress towards constitutional government. Official missions were sent out in 1906 to study foreign constitutional governments. Upon their return, they recommended Japan's system, along with a constitution, civil liberties, and a national popular assembly.

A nine-year program to prepare for self-government was announced in August 1908: advisory provincial assemblies were to be elected the next year, followed by an advisory national assembly in 1910. Suffrage was limited to educated men and those with property, and about 1,700,000 men were registered to vote. Naturally, the first elections were won primarily by representatives of the cultural, financial, and propertied elite. There were, however, few educated lawyers to help draft the necessary laws and proposed constitution.

Sun Yat-sen and the Revolution

Many republicans, socialists, radicals, and feminists came to believe their best hope was in the Revolutionary Alliance of Dr. Sun Yat-sen. He was born a peasant, educated in Hawaii, learned medicine in Hong Kong, and was forced by the plight of his nation to become a revolutionary. Following a failed attempt to seize power in Guangzhou, a price was placed on his head, and he became a traveling salesman of his radical political ideas. He fled to Japan, but made world tours to promote the revolutionary cause and to raise money. Sun was kidnapped off the streets of London by Qing agents and held prisoner in the Chinese embassy, but was released after public pressure was brought to bear.

The Revolutionary Alliance was aggressively involved in many activities within China, including organizing a mutiny in the Guangzhou New Army and a revolt in the city in 1910, both of which were suppressed.

Nationalism and the Republican Revolution

Sun was in America when he heard the revolution had begun with an accidental explosion of a bomb being constructed by revolutionary radicals in the port city of Hankou. The bomb makers were arrested and confessed. Fearing exposure, fellow revolutionists in the local New Army unit preemptively seized an ammunition depot and joined up with other rebelling soldiers to quickly seize Hankou and three nearby cities.

The rebels gained control of the middle Yangtze river. Supported by the local government, they declared Hubei province to be an independent republic. Within two months all of the southern and central provinces had declared independence from the central government.

The southern rebels prepared to made a stand against the northern New Army unit that was being sent south to confront them. Instead, the supposedly loyal northern army joined their southern compatriots in rebellion. The New Army units issued a demand for a parliament to draw up a constitution and elect a premier.

The provisional Republic of China was declared in Nanjing on January 1, 1912. Its first act was to adopt the Western calendar. Sun Yat-sen was elected president, but he stepped aside two months later when the emperor abdicated. Yuan Shikai, who commanded the northern New Army, became president. Sun encouraged the independent provinces to establish the National Assembly of the Republic of China, which moved to Beijing in May 1912.

A merger of smaller political parties formed the Chinese Nationalist Party, known as the Kuomintang, which gained a majority in the National Assembly. In July of the next year, the Kuomintang, led by Sun, attempted to overthrow Yuan. The coup was unsuccessful, and Sun once again fled to Japan.

Yuan became a virtual dictator—he declared martial law, murdered opponents, dissolved the provincial assemblies, outlawed the Kuomintang, and expelled its representatives from the National Assembly.

When World War I broke out in August 1914, Yuan declared war against Germany and seized its naval base on the Shandong Peninsula. Five months later, Japan issued its "21 Demands." These required China to vacate Shandong and transfer it to Japan, along with other land and commercial concessions. Most importantly, Japan demanded China appoint Japanese advisors in its police, military, and financial ministries. The United States and Britain advised Yuan to accede to the demands, which he did—except for the appointment of Japanese advisors. Instead of imposing a protectorate similar to what they had in Korea, the Japanese demands heightened a Chinese spirit of independence and nationalism.

Effective January 1, 1916, Yuan proclaimed a constitutional monarchy in the Empire of China, with himself as its emperor. China was once again fragmented. The South declined to be a part of Yuan's empire, and provincial leaders began to act as warlords with their own armies. Yuan renounced the empire in March and died three months later. Torn apart by competing factions, cliques, coups, and countercoups, effective central government quickly collapsed.

Warlords became the only real source of effective civil and military authority in China. As governors of provinces, with military backgrounds and commanding armies personally loyal to them, the warlords ruled their own territories. Their primary constituencies were the local conservative gentry, rather than the workers and peasants.

The May Fourth Student Movement

At the conclusion of World War I, over Chinese protests, the Paris Peace Conference decided Japan could retain the German interests it had seized on the Shandong Peninsula. The news arrived on May 4, 1919, and thousands of students waving white flags of mourning gathered in Tiananmen Square in Beijing. This protest was followed by a national boycott of Japanese goods. This became the May Fourth Movement—which rejected Confucianism and embraced new ideas. The movement ignited an explosion of nationalist literature printed in the simplified vernacular.

Students across China raised an outcry. Through speeches and printed matter, and making use of the telegraph system, they organized and made their voices heard. Some were killed and thousands were arrested, but they continued to march and demonstrate. The movement was joined by many of the newly-formed labor unions, as they all sought to slip the bonds of Confucianism and embrace their individualism.

Many people trace the beginning of modern China to this vibrant youth-led movement—which claimed participation by more than 4,500,000 Chinese students, many of whom had received western-style educations by that time.

Among the young people influenced by the May Fourth Movement were Mao Zedong, Zhou Enlai, and Deng Xiaoping—about whom we will hear more later.

Chiang Kai-shek and the Nationalists

Chiang Kai-shek was born into an upper-middle-class family of salt merchants, with strong Confucian beliefs. He was educated at the Baoding Military Academy, before attending a Japanese Army Academy Preparatory School for Chinese students. Upon graduation in 1909, Chiang served in the Japanese Army for two years.

Returning to China to participate in the 1911 revolution, Chiang led a regiment in Shanghai. He was a founding member of the Chinese Nationalist Party (Kuomintang) and, after the failed coup against Yuan, he returned to Japan. Chiang made trips back to Shanghai—which was considered the vice capital of the world. He formed a long-lasting political alliance with the notorious Green Gang, that controlled opium, prostitution, and gambling in the city.

Chiang returned to take over the Kuomintang in 1916, after its leader was assassinated by Yuan's agents. When Sun returned to China the next year to work for the reunification of China, Chiang joined forces with him. With the assistance of the local warlord in 1921, Sun established a military government in Guangzhou with himself as the Grand Marshall. In 1923, when the warlord turned on Sun, he and his wife were rescued by Chiang.

The Communist Revolution had taken place during the same time period in Russia, and one of the first acts by the Soviet government was to create the Communist International, or Comintern, to encourage, support, and control Marxist-Leninist revolutions in other countries. China was the first and primary target of the Comintern, which allocated large sums of money and installed secret agents in the major population centers of China.

After Sun recaptured Guangzhou in 1924 with the aid of Comintern agents, he sent Chiang to Russia for three months to study the Soviet system. Chiang met with Leon Trotsky and other Soviet leaders, but concluded the Russian model was not the best solution for China's problems.

Upon Chiang's return to China in 1924, he was appointed by Sun to serve as the Commandant of the Whampoa Military Academy, where he attracted a group of young officers, who became personally loyal to Chiang.

Sun's revolutionary agenda consisted of three phases. The first would be military unification, followed by political education, and, finally, by constitutional democracy. The first two stages would require a dictatorship of the Kuomintang party—much like that practiced by the Russian Communist Party. The difference being the third phase, which was imagined to be pure communism in Russia and a participatory democracy in China.

Working under the tutelage of a Russian communist agent, the Kuomintang was organized along Soviet lines, with local cells—which elected representatives to a party congress. The first congress in 1924 elected a central executive committee and accepted a constitution prepared by the Russian agent.

The Comintern's intention was to insinuate communists into the Kuomintang and to ultimately seize control. Sun believed the aims of the two groups were compatible, and communists were openly accepted for membership. At this point, the Kuomintang numbered more than 50,000 members, 500 of whom were communists.

Following a power struggle in the Kuomintang after Sun died in 1925, Chiang, as the conservative candidate, prevailed over Sun's more socialistic wing of the party. Chiang became the Commander-in-Chief of the National Revolutionary Army.

The Foundation of the Chinese Communist Party

Preceded by an interest in anarchism, socialism had earlier gained ground in China with the realization by some students they should be serving society, rather than the state. Radical groups of different ideologies and interests were regularly meeting by 1920. One such political theory was Marxism—which had found a practical expression in Russia following the February Revolution in 1917 by the Russian Communist Party, and the establishment of the Soviet Union.

The Chinese Communist Party was formed in 1920 by a group of eight young men in the home of a professor, who acted at the direction of a Comintern agent. A young teacher named Mao Zedong was acquainted with the professor; however, Mao, who had yet to accept Marxism, was not invited to the meeting.

Mao Zedong was born in 1893 in a remote valley in the center of China that was cut off from the outside world. His familial ancestors had survived by cultivating rice and tea in the valley for 500 years.

Mao's father was the most successful farmer in his village, having served as a soldier long enough to pay off his family's debts, learn to read and write, and keep accounts. He acquired more land, sold his excess produce at the market, saved his money, and built a larger house. He could afford to educate Mao, his eldest son, to be a teacher.

Shortly after the Chinese Communist Party was established, Mao was given Comintern funds by the professor to open a bookstore and distribute communist literature. These activities on behalf of the Party resulted in Mao finding a better job as the headmaster of a primary school. He thought about various "isms," including Marxism and Soviet Bolshevism, to transform China, but was not yet a member of the Communist Party or committed to its ideology. He said, "Ideas are important, but reality is even more important."

Acting under the direct control of the Comintern in Moscow, the Communist Party began to advocate aggressive action and class struggle in promulgating Marxist ideology. The Party remained a secret, highly organized, centralized group dedicated to securing the power to govern China by any means necessary, including subversion of the Nationalists and violent revolution.

Mao made his choice. He decided the fanatical terrorist tactics of the Communist Party dictatorship—with its denial of civic freedom to those outside the party—and its unwillingness to compromise, was the best solution. For him, will and power were supreme. By November 1920, he submitted to the discipline of the Communist Party and began to organize underground cells in Changsha, the capital of Hunan province, where he lived.

In 1921, two Soviet Comintern agents arrived in Shanghai to hold the Communist Party's first Congress in order to formalize its organization. Mao received an invitation and generous stipend (equal to two years of his teaching salary) to attend. From this point forward for many years, Mao was a paid agent of the Comintern and subject to its direction and discipline.

The Party congress, which consisted of 12 delegates representing 53 Chinese communists, was totally controlled by the Soviet agents. The Chinese Communist Party adopted the more radical Soviet approach, including class dictatorship, and formally united with the Comintern.

The Comintern provided the funds to operate the Party, and Mao began to receive a monthly salary. He resigned his position as headmaster to become a full-time Soviet agent. As he was less than successful in organizing workers, he was not invited to the next Party congress in 1922.

Inasmuch as the Kuomintang was the paramount political power in China and had a socialist orientation, the Comintern hedged its bets in China by providing funds to Sun and the Kuomintang, as well as the Communist Party. The Comintern sought to influence the direction and organization of the Kuomintang, and it directed its communist agents, including Mao, to openly join the Kuomintang. A high-level Comintern agent was dispatched to take control of both the Kuomintang and Communist Parties and to coordinate their activities.

Mao attended the Kuomintang's first congress in 1924 and became an alternate member of its Central Executive Committee. His exuberant promotion of Nationalist positions caused him to be criticized within the Communist Party for being too opportunistic and right wing. Mao was removed from the Communist Party's Central Committee and not allowed to attend the 1925 party congress.

When Sun died in 1925, he was temporarily replaced by Wang Jingwei, who was a member of the left wing of the Kuomintang. Drawing on Mao's enthusiastic work for the Nationalists, Wang promoted Mao into a series of high positions within the Kuomintang. Mao became Wang's assistant in the Propaganda Department and editor of the Nationalists' journal. Mao helped choose delegates for the second Kuomintang congress and delivered a major report.

In 1923, the Comintern ordered the Communist Party to place a higher priority on mobilizing China's peasantry. Continuing to work as a communist agent within the Nationalists, Mao expressed an interest in the peasant issue. In 1925, he was appointed to head the Kuomintang's Peasant Movement Training Institute, which was established with Comintern funding. The Institute began to train agents to work in the countryside to organize peasant associations and to agitate against landlords and foment peasant insurrections.

The Northern Expedition and the Communist-Nationalist Split

Initially, the communists and nationalists cooperated in the great Northern Expedition of the Revolutionary Army, as it advanced from Guangzhou to the Yangtze valley. The army consisted of 150,000 men and was supported by Russian advisors. The force divided into six main armies, which spread out across southern China. Those warlords who did not join with the Revolutionary Army were mostly defeated. Nanjing was captured in March 1927 after a fierce battle, which saw foreign residents escaping under the protection of American and British gunboats.

Exercising their increased power in the Kuomintang, the leftist and communists caused the Nationalist government to be moved from Guangzhou to Wuhan, an industrial center where the communists anticipated a greater influence among proletariat workers. The communists may have achieved some influence in the revolutionary government, but Chiang commanded the army.

Zhou Enlai had been a political officer at the Whampoa Military Academy and served as a political commissar in the Nationalist Army before Chiang Kai-shek dismissed him. Zhou was born into a family of imperial civil servants in 1898. During his education, Zhou was exposed to reformers and radicals and joined the May Fourth Movement. As an early member of the Chinese Communist Party, he lived for two years in Paris and traveled to England, before returning to China. Primarily because of his experience as a political officer and organizer, Zhou quickly rose to a leadership position in the Communist Party.

Zhou sought to install a soviet municipal government in Shanghai in 1926, and he organized 600,000 labor unionists to shut down the city with a general strike. Chiang Kai-shek called in the criminal Green Gang to slaughter labor movement activists and communists. Hundreds were killed and thousands were arrested. Among them was Zhou, who fled the city after he was released.

Continuing with the Northern Expedition, Chiang gained control over the area of Beijing and northeast China. His task was made easier after Zhang Xueliang, a powerful local warlord, declared for the Kuomintang. With this, Chiang managed to achieve a tenuous unification of China under the Nationalists—although many areas continued to be ruled by warlords. His Nationalist government was recognized by most Western powers.

The conservative Chiang had differed politically with the more liberal Sun Yat-sen; however, he honored the role Sun had played in the Revolution. Once Chiang established the Nationalist capital in Nanjing, he enshrined Sun's body in a majestic mausoleum. Chiang divorced his first wife and two concubines, and married the sister of Sun's widow.

Nationalism and the Republican Revolution

The Nationalists had profited from Comintern financial assistance and by cooperating with the Communist Party, but Chiang correctly feared the communists were trying to take over the Kuomintang. He expelled all known communists from the Kuomintang and began to suppress them in the Nationalist areas under his control. Some communists fled to Russia, but most retreated to the interior of Central China.

In his earlier role as the head of the Kuomintang Peasant Movement Training Institute, Mao had traveled into Hunan province in 1925 to witness the fruits of Institute training, and he liked what he saw. There were widespread riots as social order broke down, peasants seized property and bandits ran rampant. Mao had ordered the release of those who were arrested for the most violent acts, saying a revolution needed violence.

When Chiang began to arrest communists in 1926, Wang Jingwei, always the political opportunist, severed his connections with the Communist Party and declared his support for Chiang. Wang, who had been Mao's mentor in the Kuomintang, disavowed the rural anarchy and fired Mao. Subject to arrest, Mao fled to Hunan province.

Government by the Kuomintang

Even though Chiang Kai-shek had expelled all known communists from the Kuomintang, he still modeled the Nationalist government after the Soviet government of Russia. The Chinese Nationalist government established at Nanjing was a dictatorship under the control of Chiang and governed by the Central Executive Committee of the Kuomintang. The Committee chose the officials of the Nationalist ministries and made all major decisions. Essentially, the Kuomintang Party and the Nationalist government were one and the same.

Chiang called for a "New Life," and relying on Confucian principles, he called for discipline, decorum, and loyalty. Confucius's birthday was declared a public holiday.

Although the Kuomintang had broken away from the communists and was nominally a conservative (quasi-fascist) government, it failed to support the businesses that had blossomed—particularly those in the treaty ports. Chiang used violence and intimidation to coerce funds for the Nationalists and boycotted businesses that failed to support him. He closed the Chambers of Commerce and closely regulated the merchant class. The most successful businesses, however, were the banks that loaned money to Chiang.

With his banishment of communists and leftists from the party, Chiang lost the energy they had brought to the movement. The Nationalist government had some young professionals from the May Fourth Movement, but it also contained a lot of deadwood left over from the Qing bureaucracy and others serving in the warlord-controlled provinces. Many of these lazy officials were in office to get rich, rather than to serve the public.

Chiang personally controlled the Military Affairs Commission, which consumed half of the government's financial resources. He employed German advisors and began to seek military and industrial assistance from Germany.

Chiang became more openly fascist, creating an organization of loyal army officers known as the Blue Shirts. He used the organization in opposition to his own government whenever it suited his needs. Were it not for the attack by Japan that drew him into World War II on the side opposed to fascism, Chiang may well have found himself allied with the Axis.

Mao Hijacks the Red Army and Becomes a Bandit

Once Chiang expelled the communists from the Kuomintang and began to violently suppress the Communist Party, USSR dictator Joseph Stalin ordered the Comintern to create a Red Army in China to fight against the Nationalists and seize territory in preparation for a communist revolution.

The initial plan devised by the Comintern was for Nationalist Army units heavily infiltrated by communists to mutiny and form the nucleus of the Red Army. One such group in Jiangxi province, consisting of 20,000 Nationalist

Nationalism and the Republican Revolution

soldiers, was organized by Zhou Enlai to rebel in August 1927. The plan was to march the new Red Army through the south of Hunan province to the coast, where they would receive a shipment of weapons from Russia.

Mao, who had fled to Hunan and had nothing to do, wanted this new Red Army for his own purposes. He engaged in a devious plan to bring the army to him and take control of it. First, he pretended to need assistance to organize a peasant uprising in Hunan province. Marching without supplies, the Red Army lost almost half of its force by the time it arrived in Hunan.

Changing his mind, Mao then said he wanted to attack the city of Changsha—where he formerly lived. After the new plan was approved and he was made head of a Front Committee with authority to make tactical decisions, Mao issued orders to the Red Army to abandon the planned attack. He then marched the remaining 1,500 hungry, thirsty, and exhausted troops south into an area controlled by bandits.

Mao provided rifles to the bandit leaders and made a truce with them. When he announced yet another plan for the remnants of the Red Army to become bandits, more than half of his army deserted, leaving him with 600 soldiers. Within a short period, Mao defeated the other local bandits and captured a county seat. He organized a massive rally of peasants and ordered the mob to use their traditional spears to kill the county executive.

Having lied to the Communist Party leadership and commandeered the Red Army, Mao disobeyed orders to appear and explain his actions. He was discharged from all positions of authority. Unfazed, Mao designated himself as Division Commander of his bandit army. His military opportunism became known in Party circles as "Mao Zedongism," and his army was called "semi-bandits" in Comintern communiqués.

As a bandit chieftain, Mao lived in several spacious mansions in towns, while his army roamed the countryside on looting expeditions. He had a large personal staff, including secretaries, cooks, and a groom for his horse.

In April 1928, Mao was joined by Zhu De, who commanded another rebel army consisting of former Nationalists, who had accepted communism. Other Communist Party attempts to organize armed resistance had failed, and Mao's bandit army became the only communist army functioning, with a combined force of 5,000 men.

Mao announced he was the political commissar, and Zhu was the commander of the Zhu-Mao Army. Under the system adopted from the USSR, Party commissars existed throughout the Red Army and shared power with military officers. Commissar were responsible for ideology and party discipline and had the authority to overrule unit commanders.

A letter was sent to the Communist Party headquarters by Mao demanding an appointment to a Party leadership position. The letter was forwarded to Moscow, with Zhou Enlai's report that Mao's troops had the character of bandits. Stalin decided that—even though Mao was acting like a bandit—he did have an army and a base. Mao won this round in his battle with the central Chinese Communist Party leadership. He was officially placed in political charge of the Red Army and the surrounding area, with Zhu as the military commander.

Mao and Zhu were forced to flee from an approaching Nationalist Army, leaving their wounded behind to be slaughtered by the local citizenry-who had been terrorized by Mao's army. Zhu's wife was captured during the retreat and executed by the Nationalists. Utterly without sympathy, Mao stripped Zhu of his command and took full control of the Red Army.

After capturing a regional city in Fujian province, Zhu, with the support of the Red Army rank and file, confronted Mao and voted him out of his political post. Zhu regained command of the army.

By an amazing exercise of machination, intrigue, violence, and deception, Mao was able to regain his political power. He once again set out to deprive Zhu of his military command. In doing so, he relied on Lin Biao, one of Zhu's officers. Lin denied tactical support to Zhu during an attack by Nationalist forces, thereby putting the lives of Red Army soldiers at risk. Zhu managed to prevail in the battle, but lost the political war with Mao, who had regained the support of Zhou Enlai and Moscow.

Nationalism and the Republican Revolution

The son of a prosperous factory owner, Lin Biao studied under Chiang Kai-shek and Zhou Enlai at the Whampoa Military Academy. Following his graduation, Lin was commissioned as an officer in the Nationalist Army and participated in the Northern Expedition. He was quickly promoted to command a battalion, before becoming a communist and joining up with Zhu. Once he arrived in Jiangxi province, Lin Biao cast his lot with Mao.

Having suffered being voted out of office by Zhu and his army supporters, Mao labeled voting as "ultra-democracy" and eliminated it in his command. In addition, to defeat protests about his abuse of privilege, Mao coined the term "absolute egalitarianism" to chastise those who believed rank should not have special privileges in the Communist Party and Red Army.

With his regained political power, Mao conducted a bloody purge against what he labeled as "anti-Bolsheviks" in the Red Army. He claimed to have discovered more than 4,400, most of whom were killed after torture. Mao then turned on the local Communist Party cadres, before he was stopped by a mutiny among his troops.

The soldiers accused Mao of wanting to become the "Party Emperor," and said he was "extremely devious and sly, selfish, and full of megalomania." Even though the complaints were reported to Party headquarters, and were acknowledged to be true, Mao continued to have the support of the Party leadership and Stalin. The mutineers were labeled as counter-revolutionaries and were ordered to submit to Mao. To instill terror, Mao assembled crowds for the public executions of many of the mutineers. Ten thousand Red Army soldiers died in the purge, many after the most terrible forms of torture.

Sixty years later, in 1991, the official *History of the Communist Party* reported: "There was never an AB [anti-Bolshevik] clique in the Communist Party, and the so-called AB members were the result of torture."

To defend against attacks by the Nationalist Army, Mao relied on this strategy: "The enemy advances, we retreat; the enemy camps, we harass;

the enemy tires, we attack; the enemy retreats, we pursue." In addition, the Red Army was aided by a Russian spy in Chiang Kai-shek's group of German advisors who obtained and turned over Nationalist Army's radio codes and attack plans.

Mao absorbed two major attacks by making the communist area an unoccupied wasteland without any means of survival. The third attack was more successful, and Mao was forced to withdraw into a severely reduced area. On September 18, 1931, the Japanese invaded Manchuria—just as Chiang was prepared to finish off Mao's Red Army.

Chiang Kai-shek immediately withdrew the Nationalist Army and asked the Communist Party to establish a United Front to fight the Japanese. Chiang's overture was rejected by the Communist Party—which continued to see the defense of Russia (in case it was attacked by Japan) as the primary mission of the Red Army.

The Communist Party reoccupied the areas it had lost to the Nationalist Army and proclaimed the Chinese Soviet Republic, with its capital at Ruijin in the province of Jiangxi. Mao was appointed President and Prime Minister. He also became the chairman of the Central Executive Committee and the People's Committee. Moscow moderated Mao's power by assigning Zhu De as commander of the Red Army and Zhou Enlai as the political Party Chief, with authority over Mao. The Chinese Republic was subordinate to the Communist Party—which was a branch of the Soviet Union Comintern.

Zhou had already created the Chinese KGB, known as the Political Security Bureau—which was directly supervised by the Soviet Union KGB. Through a bewildering collection of committees in every village and hamlet, Zhou organized the entire population in the area of the Soviet Republic to be under the direct control of the Communist Party. It was the job of the Party to rule, and it was the task of the ruled to provide the Party with food and supplies, fines and donations, corvée labor, and army conscripts. As most young men were conscripted into the army or for labor, daily work for survival fell upon the women. Mao said, "Rely overwhelming on women to do farm work."

Nationalism and the Republican Revolution

Communist cadres searched out and confiscated all property belonging to the landlord class and either killed owners or sentenced them to "do endless forced labor" until death. Villages became prisons, with passes required to get past sentries. Attempted escape resulted in the death sentence, and a successful escape shifted the death sentence to the jailer or sentry. Visitors were not allowed to stay the night, and violators were killed.

The communist Soviet Republic occupied most of Jiangxi and Fujian provinces between 1931 and 1935, during which time the population decreased by 20 percent. Since escapes were so difficult, as many as 700,000 people may have died. In 1983, the Communist Party admitted that 238,844 people in Jiangxi province alone had died in the revolution and purges.

In April 1932, the Chinese Soviet Republic declared war on Japan. With reservation, however, the declaration stated, "to fight the Japanese imperialists, it is necessary first of all to overthrow the rule of the Nationalist."

With the collaboration of Lin Biao, Mao was able to scheme his way back into control of part of the Red Army. He organized a successful attack on the major city of Zhangzhou in May 1932, while Chiang was distracted by the Japanese.

Even though Mao carried off a truck load of personal loot from Zhangzhou and lost thousands of soldiers to summer heat and battles as they returned to Jiangxi province, Moscow promoted him to be the chief political commissar of the Red Army. Perhaps in Mao's lies, love of violence, and lack of concern for the health and well-being of his own soldiers, Stalin had found a soul mate. In return, Mao remained loyal to Stalin and the Comintern until Stalin's death.

Chiang Kai-shek had been unable to defend Zhangzhou against Mao's attack because of the concurrent Japanese attack on Shanghai. The Communist Party continued to expand the areas under its control forcing Chiang to return to his "Domestic Stability First" policy and renew his offensive against the communists.

Chiang first struck and captured two communist areas north of Jiangxi. Stalin ordered Mao to come to their aid, but he refused to do so. Mao believed it was best to withdraw and allow Chiang to exhaust his army, before attacking, but Moscow wanted a more direct response to attacks.

Mao's strategy gave rise to a series of heated discussions about how best to respond to the Nationalist attacks. Mao was denounced as being disrespectful to the Party leadership and removed from his army posts—even though he retained his titles as President and Premier of the Soviet Republic. Zhou Enlai was assigned to be the Red Army commissar. Mao took time off to "convalesce" in a large villa and continued to issue competing orders.

The leadership of the Communist Party was shaken up by the arrival of several young Moscow-trained operatives. One replaced Zhou as the Party Chairman and another took over the Premier position from Mao. These two—working closely with Zhou, as the Red Army commissar, and using improved intelligence from Soviet Union spies in the Nationalist government—began to achieve some victories defending against Nationalist Army attacks.

At the urging of the Comintern to cooperate with Mao and include him in planning, Mao was allowed to continue as President of the Soviet Republic and was, for the first time, made a full member of the Politburo. He was not, however, admitted to the more powerful Secretariat.

Having achieved a temporary truce with Japan in northern China, Chiang Kai-shek intensified his attack on the communists in Jiangxi province. Commanding a Nationalist Army numbering more than 300,000 field soldiers, using warplanes and heavy artillery, and advised by German military officers, Chiang ringed the communist-held area with a series of 15,000 blockhouses. He began to tighten his ring of blockhouses around the communists and to strike them with his hundreds of fighter bombers. Chiang intended to destroy the Red Army, as he sent wave after wave of Nationalist soldiers into the enclave in late 1934. Following each battle, Red Army officers executed their own seriously wounded soldiers to avoid having them captured and defecting to the Nationalist Army.

Nationalism and the Republican Revolution

Contrary to Mao's policy of tactical retreat, the new Communist Party leadership commanded the Red Army to defend against Nationalist attacks from trenches dug inside the lines of blockhouses.

As the Communist position became increasing untenable, the new Party leadership decided it could no longer hold the area. The Central Committee made secret plans to escape, but attempted to do so without Mao. Although a member of the Politburo, Mao was not included in the discussions.

Mao was suffering from recurrent malaria and depression. Using this as an excuse, an effort was made by the leadership to ship him to Russia for medical treatment. In the alternative, the leadership considered leaving Mao behind as the figurehead President of the shrinking soviet state.

Zhao Enlai kept Mao informed of the decisions, but Mao did not know until the last minute whether he would be allowed to leave with the others. In an attempt to gain favor, Mao turned over all of the loot he had kept hidden for two years, since shipping it back from Guangzhou.

Promising he would not make trouble, Mao was reluctantly allowed to accompany the other communists in their escape from Chiang's trap, in what has become known as The Long March. In the meantime, the Nationalist's undeclared war with Japan continued.

Japanese Aggression

The relationship between China and Japan has existed for thousands of years, as the Japanese adopted the Chinese writing characters, educated their most promising young people in China, and paid tribute to its emperors. Japan resisted two massive naval invasions by Kublai Khan in the Thirteenth Century and slowly became more independent as it evolved its Samurai Society and Bushido Code (the way of the warrior).

Encouraged by U.S. warships in 1852, the Empire of Japan opened up its culture to Western influences and began to surpass China in its industrialization and development of a modern military. Following its easy victory during the Sino-Japanese War in 1894, Japan continued to act aggressively by seeking to impose a protectorate over China during the First World War.

Similar to the Monroe Doctrine of the United States in the Americas, Japan expanded its sphere of influence in Asia during the earlier part of the Twentieth Century. The purpose of the Greater East Asia Co-Prosperity Sphere was to free Asia from Western colonial powers, secure control of natural resources for Japan's industries, and open new markets for its products.

Leading up to World War II, the aggression of Japanese military forces against China commenced with an invasion of Manchuria in 1931, followed by an attack on Shanghai the following year.

Invasion of Manchuria

The South Manchuria Railway was constructed between 1898 and 1903 by Russia pursuant to a treaty with China. Although located entirely within Imperial China, rights to the southern section in Manchuria was ceded to Japan in 1905 when it defeated Russia in the Russo-Japanese War. The 730-mile length of railway in China was operated by a Japanese corporation and enjoyed a huge success. Major facilities were established in towns along its track, which were protected by detachments of the Japanese army.

Acting independently from the Japanese central government and relying on an alleged terrorist attack on the railroad it staged as a pretext, the Japanese army launched an attack on China in Manchuria on September 18, 1931. The Japanese military had gained constitutional power over the government, and civilian ministers were powerless to stop the invasion. Additional troops were sent to Manchuria, and within a matter of days, Japanese forces captured most of the cities along the railroad. A week later, Japan controlled two provinces and the main rail lines into Korea.

The provinces in northeast China and Manchuria were controlled by Zhang Xueliang, the warlord who had allied himself with Chiang Kai-Shek and the Nationalists in 1926. Zhang supported the unification of China and was the commanding general of the Chinese army in the northeast.

On September 19, the Chinese Foreign Ministry protested the Japanese invasion and appealed to the League of Nations. The League passed a resolution on October 24, mandating withdrawal of all Japanese troops and established a buffer zone. Japan briefly respected the buffer zone, then continued its aggression.

Having earlier annexed Korea, the Japanese were able to quickly move thousands of troops from Korea into Manchuria using armored trains along captured railroads. Zhang's army vastly outnumbered the Japanese and was well supplied with aircraft and artillery. It was, however, poorly trained, improperly deployed, and permeated with Japanese agents. As the Nationalist government was also in crisis and could offer no assistance, Zhang retreated into northern China.

Chiang Kai-shek was preoccupied with an independence movement in Guangzhou and the communist revolution—which he believed was more of a threat than the Japanese. More concerned with internal pacification, Chiang did not declare war on Japan. He was criticized at a Kuomintang party conference in November for his failure to defend Manchuria. Chiang resigned as Chairman and was replaced as Premier of the Republic in December, but he retained his command of the Chinese army and overall power.

The Japanese occupied southern Manchuria and continued their invasion into northern Manchuria. Overcoming an organized Chinese defense, the Japanese were able to secure their hold on the north by February 1932. Guerilla resistance continued, and Japan was forced to maintain troops in Manchuria to pacify it.

In March 1932, the Japanese established the puppet state of Manchukuo in Manchuria. As its emperor, they installed Aisin-Gioro Puyi, the last child emperor of the Qing dynasty (Emperor Xuangtong), who had abdicated in 1912. The League of Nations refused to recognize Manchukuo as an independent nation, causing Japan to withdraw from the League in 1933.

Without the support of the United States in the League of Nations, and with England suffering an economic crisis at the time, no military force was authorized to support the League's demand that Japan withdraw from the Manchurian area of China. The dictators of Italy and Germany could not fail to notice, nor long delay their own plans for conquest.

Attack on Shanghai

Not content with the seizure of Manchuria, Japan set its sights on Shanghai, one of the largest, most successful and westernized of China's cities. Following an assault on five Japanese Buddhist monks—in an act believed to have been organized by Japanese agents—a factory was burned in Shanghai in January 1932. There was public outrage against Japan and a boycott threatened against its goods. Japan, which held a concession in the city, deployed a naval and military force to "protect" its citizens and treaty rights.

An ultimatum was presented to the city council by the Japanese, demanding compensation for property damage and suppression of anti-Japanese activities. The council agreed and bribed the Chinese Nationalist Army to not intervene—which the council believed would only make matters worse.

Despite appeasement, the Japanese launched an air attack from a carrier and bombed Shanghai. This was the first instance of a carrier-based attack and terror bombing of a civilian population—a preview of the coming horrors of World War II. The attack was followed by the invasion of 3,000 Japanese troops, which was resisted by the Chinese army.

Because of the multiple foreign concessions and investments in the city, the United States, England, and France offered to negotiate a ceasefire. Japan refused, continued to increase its concentration of troops, and issued an ultimatum for the Nationalist Army to withdraw—which was rejected.

The number of Japanese troops was increased to 90,000, supported by a massive armada of ships and airplanes. Chiang Kai-shek deployed an additional Chinese army into the battle. Fighting continued through February, but Japanese air power and the superior quality of its military caused the Chinese army to disintegrate and retreat from the city.

The League of Nations demanded a ceasefire on March 4, 1932, which was honored by China, but not Japan. Sporadic fighting continued until the League was able to negotiate the Shanghai Ceasefire Agreement in May. Shanghai became a demilitarized zone. Although China could not station troops in the area, Japan was allowed to maintain a military presence in the city alongside the Shanghai police force.

Chiang redeployed the Nationalist Army from Shanghai to resume his war against the communists. We earlier followed the progress of that civil war between the Nationalists and the Communists, up to the escape of Mao Zedong and the Red Army from the communist enclave in Jiangxi province during the late autumn of 1934.

The Long March

On October 10, 1934, approximately 86,000 Red Army soldiers, half of whom were new recruits and party cadres, assembled with the Communist Party leadership. Many of the sick, injured, elderly, and feeble were unable to leave. Most of the Red Army was going to break out, but 25,000 troops, of whom 10,000 were wounded, would remain to protect those who were left behind. A diversionary force was sent off in another direction—never to be heard from again.

At the last minute, the communists executed thousands of healthy Red Army soldiers, who were judged to be insufficiently reliable. Many of them were former Nationalist soldiers—who had to dig a large pit into which they were tossed after being killed, or in which they were buried alive.

Almost everything possessed by the Communist Party, which could be moved, was carried by thousands of hired porters. This included printing presses, machinery for making ammunition, light artillery, miles of telephone cable, gold and silver reserves, and the party's archives. Mao brought a bag of books.

Breaking Out

The initial plan was to strike west and penetrate the lines of Nationalist blockhouses and then head northwest toward another communist enclave on the Hunan-Hubei border. The Red Army was divided into two parallel columns, which protected the headquarters column and thousands of bearers in the center. The columns slipped away at night along foot paths to avoid the Nationalist fighter bombers, and they slept under cover during the day.

For several reasons, such stealth was probably unnecessary as Chiang Kai-shek was under great pressure to allow the Red Army to escape. Foremost, Chiang's only son, who had been sent by Chiang ten years earlier to study in Moscow, was being held hostage by Stalin. In addition, as Japan and Russia were in conflict over Manchuria and adjacent territory, Chiang wanted to maintain good relations with Russia. Finally, Chiang intended to use the Chinese Red Army's movement through warlord-controlled provinces as an excuse to invade his own Nationalist forces into those areas.

The Red Army crossed the lines of blockhouses at the extreme southwest of Jiangxi into Guangdong province with little difficulty. Zhou Enlai, who would become Communist China's most famous diplomat, had negotiated safe passage from the Guangdong warlord. Zhou had also obtained the Nationalist Army codebook, and the Red Army was able to intercept and decipher Chiang's radio traffic.

The columns began to openly move and fight during the day, and each night, the commanders made plans for the next day. Many of the top echelon, including Mao, slept in sling litters carried by two bearers during the march.

The only major battle during the march shaped up when the Red Army came to the point where it had to shift northward, if it were to join the communist enclave in western Hunan. Half of the Red Army had already crossed the Xiang river, when it intercepted by the Nationalists and engaged in a fierce battle. The rear columns were continually strafed by Nationalist warplanes as they approached the river, only to find the crossing blocked by a surprise attack by the local warlord.

The bloody battle continued for a week until the final elements of the army made it across the river. The Red Army managed to escape, but the communists were forced to abandon most of their archives, and 75 percent of the porters absconded. Communist Party tradition has it that more than half of the Red Army was killed at the Xiang river; however, desertions more likely accounted for a large portion of its reduced strength.

The Long March

Mao Takes Command

Arriving in Tongdao, an informal meeting was held to decide whether the army would turn north to join up with the Hunan enclave as originally planned. For the first time in more than two years, Mao was permitted to discuss an issue of major importance. He advocated the Red Army redirect its route northwest toward Guizhou, and his suggestion was accepted.

Mao's position was reinforced during a follow-up meeting of the Politburo in Liping, once they crossed the border into Guizhou. Mao proposed they head west and capture Zunyi, the second largest city in the province, and make further decisions at that time.

After engaging in two days of hard fighting, the Red Army crossed the Wu river on a bamboo pontoon bridge and pushed on toward Zuyni. They arrived at the city walls during the night of January 3, 1935. Pretending to be Nationalists pursued by the Red Army, they were allowed in the gate. By daybreak, they controlled the city.

The surrounding area was found to be too backward for the city to be used as a base, so a full meeting of the Politburo was held to choose a new destination. A watershed for the direction and control of the Revolution, the meeting was dominated by Mao and Zhou Enlai. Although technically senior to Mao, from this point forward Zhou carried Mao's water.

Zhou took responsibility for having advocated the Nationalist Army be met with force and positional trenches—which was why the communist base in Jiangxi province was lost. Mao criticized the leadership and advocated a new direction.

The meeting lasted for three evenings, while a major reorganization of the army took place during the day. Most of the heavy equipment was buried or destroyed, and 4,000 locals were recruited. A muster revealed the Red Army had been reduced to 30,000 soldiers—from the original 86,000.

Mao's star was clearly in the ascendance as the meetings continued. Zhou supported Mao's positions and nominated him to become the General Front Commander of the Red Army and a member of the Secretariat. The nominations were approved by consensus.

Keeping the minutes of these fateful meetings was Deng Xiaoping, the editor of the *Red Star* and secretary of the Central Committee. Deng had earlier been criticized, in part for having supported Mao, and removed from Party positions. His wife had divorced him, and he started the march carrying his own equipment.

Deng's father was a middle-class landowner with a college education. Following his own mid-level education, Deng traveled to Paris at age 15 as a participant in a work-study program. He met Zhou Enlai, and under his influence, Deng became a member of the Communist Party. Both Zhou and Deng would become key supporters of Mao Zedong throughout their lives.

The Long March would continue, and the path ahead would be difficult and dangerous, but a new leader was in charge. The decision was made to connect with the Communist Fourth Army in Sichuan by moving far to the west in order to cross the upper waters of the Yangtze river at its western extension, known as the Golden Sands River.

As Mao ducked and weaved along the army's path towards the river crossing, he created diversions to confuse the Nationalist Army. Chiang was less than vigorous at trapping Mao in the rich heartland of China, in his scheme to drive the Red Army to a more remote corner of China with fewer resources and less population.

Crossing the Yangtze

Upon arrival at the ancient river crossing of the Golden Sands River, the Red Army quickly disarmed the guards, seized funds from the customs office and secured enough boats and boatmen to move the communist troops across the river in a continuous flow during nine days and nights in May 1935.

On the other side, the Red Army attacked a local defense battalion dug in on top of a mastiff known as the Lion's Head. Advancing under a hail of bullets and rolled boulders, the bugle sounded and the communists charged, shouting "Kill! Kill! Kill! The defenders fled, and the Red Army, reduced to 25,000 troops, was north of the Yangtze river.

Their trip northward would not be easier than the arduous path they had already traveled. Although the communists would encounter fewer

Nationalist troops, the route would be far more physically challenging. Moreover, while the communists had been receiving some support from Han people along their march, the way ahead was populated with unsympathetic Tibetans and the Yi people.

The Red Army entered the land of Yi, a slave and bandit society from the area of Burma and Tibet. Based on thousands of years of conflict, the Yi hated the Chinese. Mao found his way blocked by hundreds of Yi, who demanded money. After handing over some silver coins, the communists were told they still could not pass through. Following negotiations, an army officer became a blood brother of the local chief, and the main body of the Red Army was allowed to pass. Army stragglers, however, were robbed, stripped of their clothing and left to die.

Fable of the Luding Suspension Bridge

One remaining obstacle was the Dadu river, which had to be crossed over the high, iron, 13-chain suspension bridge at Luding that connected the cliffs on each side. The bridge was usually guarded by a Nationalist detachment armed with machine guns; however, the Nationalist force had been withdrawn and the bridge was easily crossed.

Communist Party lore claims a Red Army suicide force charged through flames and machine gun fire to seize the bridge. In fact, there were no casualties. Deng Xiaoping, who was present, later confirmed the "heroic attack" on the bridge was a dramatization for propaganda purposes.

Although no longer pursued by Nationalist troops, the Army still had to cross the perilous Great Snowy Mountains before meeting up with the Fourth Front Army, hopefully approaching from another direction. Radio communications had been spotty, and both armies were on the move.

Crossing the Great Snowy Mountains

Ahead was a 14,000-foot pass through the Jiajin Mountains. Most of the Red Army soldiers came from the hot and humid south and were inexperienced with cold weather. Few had warm clothing; they wore straw sandals and each carried about 25 pounds of gear. The air was freezing and thin at the top of the pass. Due to the lack of oxygen, any delay would be deadly. The way up and over was slow and steady, with men holding hands to keep from falling.

Just beyond the highest mountain pass was the town of Dawei, where advance parties from the two armies finally connected. Continuing, Mao made his way to Lianghekou to meet up with Zhang Guotao (Chang Kuo-tao), who commanded the Fourth Front Army. Consisting of 80,000 soldiers and 70,000 noncombatants, the Fourth vastly outnumbered Mao's much diminished First Front Army.

Zhang was one of the 12 founders of the Chinese Communist Party, he had chaired the first Party congress in 1921 attended by Mao. As a member of the Secretariat, Zhang did not hold Mao in high esteem.

Internal Conflict

With Zhou Enlai presiding, a meeting of the Politburo was held on June 26. Mao proposed the combined armies continue north where they could find Han Chinese support and make contact with the Soviet Union. Zhang wanted to move west into Tibetan territory. Mao prevailed and Zhang became vice-chairman of a unified command. The combined armies moved on through the Great Snowy Mountains.

Zhang replaced Zhou, who was serious ill, as the Chief Commissar of the Red Army and vice-chairman of the Military Commission. Zhang was put in command of the unified force, while Mao retained leadership of the Communist Party.

A compromise was reached to split into two columns, with a blending of military forces and political cadres. The Left Column primarily contained Zhang's Fourth Front Army personnel. The Right had the remains of Mao's First Front Army, augmented with additional troops. Zhou and the former headquarters group were with the Mao's Right Column. Zhang commanded both columns, and he proposed to march with the Left in the direction of Aba in the direction of Tibet. Mao accused Zhang of wanting to take the easy road and, on behalf of the political leadership, ordered Zhang to follow the Right column.

Crossing the Grasslands

It was the rainy season, and ahead of the Right Column lay the Grasslands, a vast swampy marshland. A direct crossing took five to seven days. There was no food along the way, no dry ground on which to build cooking fires or to sleep, and the water was poisonous to drink. The first units were able to follow marked trails laid down by scouts, but the trails were quickly beaten down into watery ditches. The bog acted as quicksand, and many who fell could not be rescued. Hundreds died. Mao was carried through on his litter, but had to abandon some of his books.

The Right Column struggled out of the Grasslands to a small Tibetan town, where they paused. They received a radio message that the Left Column had entered the Grasslands, but had stopped at a river where their progress was halted by the high waters. Zhang proposed to return to Aba and wait for the flood to subside.

Splitting the Armies

On September 8, Zhang sent a coded secret message to a loyal aide in Mao's group ordering the Right Column to reverse direction and return through the Grassland for a meeting to resolve differences. The message was intercepted and decoded by a Mao loyalist and taken to Mao. Claiming Zhang had ordered his men to capture the party leadership, Mao secretly caused his First Front Army troops to be rounded up, and they quickly departed during the night, leaving the Zhang loyalists behind.

Mao was the political commissar of a much reduced army, which was split in three columns. One column was commanded by Lin Biao, who had earlier conspired with Mao in Jiangxi province to usurp Zhu De.

Arrival in Shaanx

The way was clear for Mao and his Red Army to enter southern Gansu province. Upon their arrival, they read in Chinese newspapers that Liu Zhidan had established a communist base in northern Shaanx province. This became Mao's final destination.

Mao and his Red Army of 4,000 arrived in northeast Shaanx in October 1935. One year and 5,000 miles had passed since they left Jiangxi, having marched an average of 14 miles per day. Due to casualties and desertions, there were more political cadres (or officers) than soldiers. Many of those who survived the march were destined to lead the Communist Revolution and govern the People's Republic of China for the remainder of their lives.

Within months, Liu Zhidan and his top two commanders were killed under suspicious circumstances, and there was no one left to challenge Mao's command of the combined Red Army.

Mao considered his command of the Red Army to be more important than holding Party positions. He preached, "Political power grows out of the barrel of a gun."

The primary beneficiary of the march was Mao, whom Stalin proclaimed to be the political boss of the Chinese Communist Party and leader of the Chinese people. Stalin sent an order to Mao to move closer to the border to help protect the USSR against Japan.

The United Front

Mao moved to Yan'an, a city in northern Shaanxi province in 1937, where he remained for the next ten years. From there, he directed the Red Army's limited participation in the war against Japan and the subsequent communist revolution against the Nationalist government.

Ultimately, the Communist Party assembled most of its Red Army in the far northwest under Mao's command. Chiang Kai-shek remained intent on defeating the communists, rather than the Japanese. He believed the Japanese "were a disease of the skin, while the communists were a disease of the heart." Chiang ordered the former warlord Zhang Xueliang,

The Long March

who commanded the Nationalist Army in North China, to defeat Mao's forces.

Zhang made his headquarters in Xi'an, capital of Shaanxi province where Mao had taken up residence. Zhang—who had designs to succeed Chiang Kai-shek in leading the Nationalist government—began secret negotiations with Russian diplomats in Shanghai and Nanjing regarding his and Mao's situations. In addition, he contacted Mao's headquarters.

Moscow ordered Mao to treat Chiang as an ally and to form an alliance to fight the Japanese—who continued to threaten Russia on its eastern Siberian border. Stalin sent Mao the first installment of American dollars, but a shipment of weapons and other supplies directly from the USSR across the Mongolian border was intercepted by the Nationalist Army.

Zhang saw a way to help Russia, the Chinese Communist Party, and his own chances to take over the Nationalist government. When Chiang flew to Xi'an in October 1936 to coordinate plans against the Red Army, Zhang tried to convince him to join forces with the communists to meet the impending invasion by Japan. Chiang was not receptive, and at a subsequent December meeting in Xi'an, Zhang killed Chiang's bodyguards and arrested him.

Zhang asked the Communist Party to send representatives to Xi'an to discuss the fate of Chiang and China. Mao wanted Chiang executed for his crimes, while Zhou Enlai argued this fate would harm their cause in the West. Stalin ordered consultations and Mao agreed.

A communist delegation was sent to Xi'an and negotiated an agreement to form a united front against Japan. Chiang was released, and Zhang escorted him back to Nanjing. Zhang was tried in a military court and sentenced to ten years in prison. Chiang commuted the sentence, but kept Zhang under house arrest for most of his life—even after the Nationalist exodus to Taiwan.

In order to secure an invitation from Chiang for Zhou Enlai to travel to Nanjing for direct negotiations, Stalin promised he would release Chiang's son. After eleven years in Russia, the boy was returned in April 1937.

Zhou negotiated a Second United Front with Chiang in 1937, under which the Communist Party agreed to stop the revolution and its land confiscation and redistribution program. The Nationalists agreed to stop attacking the communists and to release all political prisoners. Both sides promised to concentrate their efforts on defeating the Japanese. Shortly thereafter, Japan invaded China.

Chiang Kai-shek had not declared war on Japan after it conquered Manchuria in 1932, nor after Japan occupied Shanghai the next year. In fact, Chiang would not formally declare war on Japan until after the United States entered the war following the Japanese attack on Pearl Harbor.

Nonetheless, once Japan launched its war of conquest in July 1937, Chiang knew he had to demonstrate his ability to resist the Japanese—if he were to receive help from the West. Japan's propaganda claimed it could conquer Shanghai in three days and China in three months. The task would not be nearly so easy, even though the Japanese deployed some of the terrible weapons and practices that came to characterize the horrendous world war that followed.

World War

Known in China as the War of Resistance Against Japan, the flames leading to the inferno of World War II were ignited by the Japanese invasion of Manchuria and the attack on Shanghai. Dissatisfied with the proceeds of their initial aggression, the Japanese military sought to conquer all of China.

Following its annexation of Manchuria, the Japanese invaded the area north of Beijing and seized the province of Jehol. In its North China Autonomous Movement, Japan subverted local warlords and installed collaborators to take control of five additional northern provinces. It established "autonomous councils" in these areas and stationed troops to defend industrial and railroad concessions. By 1936, the Nationalist government no longer possessed government authority in most of northern China, although it continued to control Beijing.

During the night of July 7, 1937, there was a misunderstanding between Japanese and Nationalist troops over training maneuvers at the Marco Polo railroad bridge—which controlled access to Beijing, a few miles to the east. This led to the first shots being fired in the long-anticipated war of conquest.

Japan continued its hard line, and Chiang Kai-shek was pressured by public opinion to finally take a stand against Japanese aggression. He did, and during the next eight years 20 million Chinese died, 95 million were forced from their homes, and property valued at $383 billion was destroyed.

The Battle of Shanghai

Shanghai was China's largest city and a showcase of modernization, banking, and commerce. It was also at the mouth of the Yangtze river, upstream of which lay China's most important industrial and economic heartland, its capital city of Nanjing, and the major city of Wuhan. Chiang drew the line against further appeasement and retreat in Shanghai, saying, "If we allow one more inch of our territory to be lost, we shall be guilty of an unpardonable crime against our race."

The battle for Shanghai commenced on August 14, 1937, when the Nationalist air force attacked the Japanese navy in Shanghai harbor. The Nationalists had the largest army and German-trained divisions, but the Japanese had complete naval authority. Although it faced some resistance, Japan used carrier-based fighters and land-based bombers to largely destroy China's air force and achieve air superiority.

Eventually, the Japanese landed more than 200,000 troops, supported by tanks and heavy artillery, in or near Shanghai. The Nationalist Army engaged in a fierce resistance, including suicide attacks by "dare to die" volunteers strapped with explosives—who threw themselves under tanks. As the battle extended beyond Shanghai into the surrounding cities and towns, the Chinese often fought to the last man, without surrendering.

The Japanese made additional landings in an attempt to encircle the remaining Nationalist Army, but Chiang retreated in the direction of Nanjing. The battle for Shanghai had lasted for almost three months, instead of the three days predicted by the Japanese. At the cost of hundreds of thousands of Chinese soldiers, the battle demonstrated to the West that the Chinese could resist, and it allowed time for Chiang Kai-shek to ship war materials and the most vital industries up the Yangtze river.

The battle did not, however, lead to the imposition of any sanctions by the Western powers against Japan. China's appeal to the League of Nations in September resulted only in the League's "spiritual support." A Nine-Power-Treaty Conference was convened in Brussels, but it adjourned without making any recommendation or taking any action. Preoccupied with the German threat, England recognized Japan's occupation of China, and the United States continued to do business with the Japanese.

The Rape of Nanjing

It took less than a month for the Japanese invasion force to reach Nanjing, having overcome three hardened defense rings around the city. Realizing he could not defend the city and not wanting to risk the remainder of his most effective troops, Chiang left the defense of Nanjing to 100,000 untrained and poorly armed troops.

The city was assaulted by a force of 350,000 Japanese and overrun in December 1937. In what has become known as the Rape of Nanjing, the Japanese slaughtered more than 300,000 Chinese civilians and raped thousands of women.

At this point, Chiang had lost more than half of his best-trained troops and officers. What he had hoped would be an effective fighting force had been decimated in the Battles of Shanghai and Nanjing.

The Battle of Wuhan

After the fall of Shanghai and Nanjing, Wuhan, the second largest city in China with a population of two million, became the political and industrial center of China. Located upstream at the intersection of the Yangtze and Han rivers, it was one of the most ancient and civilized cities in China.

The Japanese conquest of Wuhan would take even longer than Shanghai, becoming one of the largest battles in history. Chiang attempted to slow down the invasion by ordering the dikes of the Yellow river to be broken. A half-million Chinese civilians died in the flood—without significantly delaying the Japanese advance.

The assault on Wuhan began with major air attacks, which were fought off by the remaining Nationalist Chinese air force. Russia had loaned Chiang money to purchase Russian tanks, artillery, and 1,000 airplanes. Ultimately, as many as 2,000 Russian "volunteer" pilots shot down 1,000 Japanese planes.

The battle for Wuhan commenced with a river-borne naval assault on June 13, 1936, which was coordinated with a land attack by the main force of the Japanese military. As in Shanghai, the Nationalist Chinese conducted an all-out defense, requiring the Japanese to commit troops from its mainland and Russian border areas.

Pursuant to the Second United Front agreement, the Communist Party created the New Fourth Army in Jiangxi province, Mao's former base. Zhou Enlai was present in Wuhan, and 10,000 Red Army soldiers fought alongside the Nationalist Army in its defense.

In addition to its technological advantages in airpower, armor, and artillery, Japan employed chemical weapons, including poisonous gas, against the Chinese on at least 375 occasions in the battle for Wuhan. This use was condemned by the League of Nations in 1938.

Following one of the bloodiest battles in history, Chiang was once again forced to retreat to avoid encirclement. As he left to move his industry and government further up the Yangtze, the dead bodies of 107,000 Japanese soldiers, 225,000 Chinese soldiers, and an untold number of Chinese civilians littered the battlefield.

Retreat to Chongqing

Chiang continued to trade space for time, as he retreated further up the Yangtze River above the Three Gorges to the city of Chongqing (Chungking). Here he would remain for the duration of the war. Even though the city suffered repeated bombings, it was not attacked by land. Unable to dislodge the Nationalist Army, the Japanese resorted to massive terror bombing of the population centers in Chongqing, killing millions of civilians.

The Japanese managed to occupy all of the major cities along the coast of China and in the areas of northern China it had earlier secured. In spite of its use of biological and chemical weapons, including ceramic bombs filled with fleas carrying bubonic plague, Japan had little success in taking inland cities and failed to conquer the vast interior of China.

The Puppet Government
After Japan occupied Guangzhou, Wang Jingwei, the ultimate opportunist and Mao's former Kuomintang mentor, defected to the Japanese. Wang established a collaborationist government in Nanjing for the remainder of the war.

To the limited extent possible, Japan controlled interior areas through Wang's puppet government. He deployed a collaborationist Chinese army to provide security in the occupied areas. Nonetheless, both the Nationalists and the Communists conducted guerilla warfare throughout the occupied areas.

Allied With the United States
The north, coastal, and Yangtze river areas of China were lost and much of the balance was controlled by warlords. Chiang actually governed very little, and he became dependent on outside resources for survival. Initially, supplies were received from Russia through the northwest province of Xinjiang, which was ruled by a pro-Soviet warlord. The supplies stopped when Russia signed the Soviet-Japanese Neutrality Pact in April 1941.

Even before Pearl Harbor was attacked, the United States, England, and France were providing loans and war supplies to China. Ten thousand tons of supplies were shipped each month by rail through Vietnam. Once Japan conquered Vietnam, supplies were redirected through Burma—until it, too, was invaded. Thereafter, until the Burma Road was recaptured, everything had to be flown in from India "over the hump" of the Himalayan foothills.

Within days of the Japanese attack on Pearl Harbor, China finally declared war on Japan, Germany, and Italy. China was immediately recognized as a key member of the Allied effort to defeat the Axis. Chiang

Kai-shek was made Commander-in-Chief of all Allied forces in the China theatre of World War II.

The United States had already authorized the American Volunteer Group to help replace the aircraft and crews previously supplied by Russia to China. The Flying Tigers landed after the U.S. declared war on Japan, and thereafter provided air services in defense of China.

When the United States staged its first (Doolittle) bombing raid on Japan from a carrier in April 1942, 15 of the 16 aircraft landed in China after their bombing run. The American flyers were aided by the Chinese, and 14 crews ultimately managed to return to the United States. A massive Japanese search for the Americans resulted in the deaths of 250,000 Chinese.

The U.S. Army assigned four-star General Joseph Stillwell to serve as Chiang's chief of staff and to command American forces in China, Burma, and India. As General Eisenhower was doing in Europe, Stillwell wanted to take overall command of the allied forces and pursue an aggressive attack strategy.

Once the flow of supplies through Burma was blocked by the Japanese, Chiang choose to remain on the defensive until the blockade could be broken. This was especially true following the devastating losses suffered by the Nationalists during Japan's Ichigo offensive in 1944 that drove deep into Nationalist territory. Moreover, Chiang planned to preserve his military capacity—waiting for the U.S. to defeat Japan—in order to resume his war against the communists.

Given the institutional corruption and inefficiency of the Nationalist Government, Stillwell had little confidence in the ability of the Nationalist Army to conduct an offensive war against the Japanese on the Chinese mainland. This is one reason why the United States decided to spearhead its attack from the southern Pacific Ocean through Japan's island defenses. The primary role of the Nationalist Army was to tie up Japanese forces in China, preventing them from being redeployed against the amphibious invasions of the Japanese-held islands.

Pursuant to the United Front agreement, Zhou Enlai served as the deputy director of the Nationalist Military Committee's Political

Department in both Wuhan and Chongqing. In this position, he not only coordinated the recruitment of communists throughout southern China, but he maintained liaison with Westerners—including General Stillwell.

In 1944, Zhou tried to convince Stillwell that the Communist Party desired a united government with the Nationalists following the war and asked that American supplies go directly to the communists in the northwest. When Stillwell was replaced by Roosevelt at Chiang's insistence, an agreement was made for an American military mission to be stationed at Mao's headquarters.

Mao Bides His Time

Under the United Front agreement, Mao was assigned to occupy and control a large area having a population of two million, with Yan'an as its capital. Chiang armed and paid for 46,000 regular Red Army troops.

Mao resided in several large mansions which had been abandoned when the wealthy owners fled from the Red Army. He had a personal American doctor, and senior Communist Party cadres received special hospital treatment. All others had to receive permission for medical care from their work units.

Different levels of food, clothing, tobacco, paper, and candles were provided by the Party—depending on one's status. The children of the top echelon were sent to Russia to study or had nannies assigned to care for them. The leadership made its case for such special privileges by saying they were forced to accept them by order of the Party.

Pursuant to the agreement under the United Front, the Red Army participated in the Battle of Tai'erzhuang—the first major victory against the Japanese in January 1938. Red Army units coordinated a frontal attack with the Nationalist Army and sabotaged a railroad, cutting off Japanese supplies. The Japanese were encircled and defeated, with the fierce participation of Nationalist suicide units which disabled Japanese tanks.

The Red Army initiated a Hundred Regiments Offensive in August 1940 that cut railroads and destroyed blockhouses throughout northern

China. Initially it was a great victory, but the Japanese responded with more troops, ordered to "kill all, burn all, loot all." From then on, the Japanese did not discriminate between the military or civilians and destroyed everything they encountered.

The United Front broke down in January 1941 after Mao deliberately caused the slaughter of 2,000 members of his own New Fourth Army (N4A) by ordering it to take a route different than the one designated and protected by Chiang. The N4A encountered a much larger Nationalist force—which thought it was being attacked by the N4A. The Nationalist Army decimated the N4A over several days of battle. The N4A repeatedly radioed Mao for assistance, but Mao ignored the calls.

The Nationalist called off the slaughter, and the survivors were allowed to escape north along the originally approved route. Mao ordered Zhou Enlai to make the greatest propaganda use of the massacre and to take every diplomatic advantage of it. A publicity campaign in the West claimed 10,000 communists died in an unprovoked Nationalist attack.

Based on the alleged attack, Mao attempted to get Stalin to approve a resumption of the civil war, but Stalin ordered him to avoid a split with Chiang. To reinforce the order, Stalin reminded Mao that two of his sons were studying in Moscow.

Thereafter, Mao primarily directed limited guerrilla attacks in the areas controlled by the Red Army and engaged in widespread recruitment throughout China. Communist Party membership increased from 100,000 in 1937 to 1.2 million in 1945, and its military force grew from 92,000 to 910,000 troops.

In a secret report to Joseph Stalin in 1940, Zhou Enlai revealed that since 1937, more than a million Nationalist soldiers had died, while Red Army losses were only 40,000. After this, the communists no longer engaged in major military battles. They limited themselves to guerilla warfare in order to preserve and increase their strength for resumption of the civil war.

In 1943, Mao designated Liu Shaoqi as his second in command. Liu was born into a wealthy peasant family in 1898 and did well in school. He was selected to learn Russian and be educated by the Comintern in

Moscow. Liu returned to China to organize labor unions and head the Communist Party's Labor Department. He was elected to the Communist Party Central Committee and made the Long March as far as the Zunyi conference. From there, he was dispatched to the North to organize underground activities before rejoining Mao in Yan'an. Because of his Russian education, Liu favored the Soviet system, but he was devoted to Mao and posed no threat to his leadership.

In July 1944, the United States Army Observation Group (Dixie Mission) was deployed to Mao's headquarters. The Group's assignment was to determine if the Chinese Communist Party would be an effective military force and a reliable post-war ally.

The Dixie Mission, consisting of military and diplomatic personnel, remained with Mao for three years. American diplomat John S. Service believed the Chinese communists were similar to European socialists, rather than Russian communists. Service favorably compared the orderliness and honesty of the Communist Party to the corruption and disorder of the Nationalist government. Another foreign service officer, John Paton Davies, believed the Communist Party would be a better ally than the Kuomintang. Nonetheless, the United States continued its support of Chiang, and both of these Americans would later suffer harm to their reputations and professions because of their conclusions.

The Japanese Surrender

The United States used the atomic bomb on Hiroshima on August 6, 1945. Three days later, after another bomb was dropped on Nagasaki, the Soviet Union renounced its nonaggression treaty with Japan and declared war. Russia immediately launched a massive invasion of Manchuria and quickly overwhelmed the Japanese military forces. Japan informally surrendered, unconditionally, on August 15, 1945.

Following Japan's formal surrender on September 2, 1945, General Douglas MacArthur ordered all Japanese forces in China, except Manchuria, to surrender to Chiang Kai-shek—which they did on September 9.

The Soviet Union's occupation of Manchuria lasted long enough for it to remove much of the Japanese industrial equipment and to allow Mao's Red Army to enter and arm itself with the surrendered Japanese weapons and hardware. The communists quickly took control of the countryside in North China and surrounded Nationalist forces in the cities.

The war against the Japanese had ended, but the War of Liberation was just beginning.

Mao Establishes a Dynasty

World War II ended with a Communist Party dictatorship in northern China and a Nationalist dictatorship in southern China. The most wishful thinking in Washington, DC was that the two dictators could unite in a freely elected coalition government. Should that not be possible, the United States would support Chiang Kai-shek for a while longer.

Acting on America's encouragement, Chiang Kai-shek invited Mao Zedong and Zhou Enlai to Chongqing for a peace conference. With Zhou attending to the details, Chiang and Mao met 11 times over 43 days to negotiate a solution to their differences. There was no agreement, and Mao returned to Yan'an in October 1945. Zhou remained to work on a joint resolution for another month, but fighting had resumed by the time he rejoined Mao.

The United States deployed 53,000 Marines to Beijing and Tianjin to warn off any Soviet designs in northern China. America also transported Nationalist troops by air and sea to occupy Manchurian cities.

President Harry S. Truman dispatched U.S. Army General George C. Marshall to China as his special envoy in December 1945 to negotiate a ceasefire and unity government. After Marshall met with Chiang in Chongqing and consulted with Mao in Yan'an, the parties agreed to a ceasefire. Marshall convened a Political Consultative Conference in Beijing to negotiate a unified government.

Neither party would agree to a unity government on terms acceptable to the other during negotiations that lasted for a year, and both used the time to improve their military and political positions. Marshall, unused to failure, returned empty-handed to the United States in February 1947. In his report, he stated "The greatest obstacle to peace has been the complete, almost overwhelming suspicion with which the Chinese Communist and the Guomindang [Kuomintang] regard each other."

The Dixie Mission remained with Mao in Yan'an, and one of its final assignments was to host another special envoy from President Truman. Lieutenant General Albert Wedemeyer—who had replaced General Stillwell in China—arrived in July 1947 on a fact-finding mission. Upon his return, Wedemeyer recommended extensive training and assistance for the Nationalist Army. Truman suppressed Wedemeyer's report and imposed an embargo on further military shipments to Chiang. It was this action, primarily, that led to the Republican Party charge that Truman (and General Marshall—who had become Truman's Secretary of State) "lost China."

The Seventh Chinese Communist Party Congress in April 1945 was conducted under a sign reading, "March Forward Under the Banner of Mao Zedong." For the first time, Mao became chairman of all three of the top Party governing bodies: the Central Committee, the Politburo, and the Secretariat. His power over the Communist Party, and the government it established for China, was unprecedented and has never since been equaled. For the next 31 years Chairman Mao was one and the same as the government of China.

Mao Zedong Thought

Marxism is a complicated economic and philosophical theory, which is difficult to comprehend in any language and impossible to effectively apply in any political circumstance. In essence, Marxism envisions that all human societies pass through certain defined economic phases as they travel to a pure communistic utopia. As the different classes of society struggle with each other, they ultimately arrive at a place where there are no classes. Indeed, there is no state, nor government, and everything is owned in common by everyone. Everyone is equal and equally gifted with knowledge, wisdom, ambition, and emotional stability. Thus, all political and economic decisions on what to do and how to do it are made by a free association of everyone—in which the thoughts and opinions of everyone has equal weight and influence. The final bliss is, as stated by Karl Marx, "From each according to his ability, to each according to his needs." In other words, once a society evolves to pure communism, it easily produces enough goods and services to satisfy everyone's needs. Getting there, and who's in charge along the way, is the big problem.

Again as an oversimplification, Marx taught that through a series of revolutions, societies evolve from slavery, to feudalism, to bourgeois (merchants-owners-employers) capitalism, to socialism, and finally to pure communism. As a scientific theory, every stage has to be accounted for, or else it doesn't work out.

In Russia, Vladimir Lenin found a serf society that was hardly out of the feudal stage and barely entering bourgeois capitalism. Nonetheless, in what became known as Leninism, he held that capitalism had to be destroyed through a revolution by the proletariat (workers-employees). The revolution was led by a vanguard party (the Bolsheviks), who were sufficiently intelligent and politically aware to teach the proletariat how to achieve class consciousness.

Lenin did not believe capitalism could reform itself. The party would establish a state dictatorship to develop and construct socialism as a means to achieve pure communism. All property and means of production would be owned and managed by the state, without the need for money. Finally, the party-operated dictatorship would be democratically governed by workers through local party councils known as soviets.

We have now lived long enough to see that Marxism-Leninism did not work. The Soviet Union dissolved in 1991, and Russia adopted capitalism. Perhaps Marx was right, and capitalism *is* an essential phase, having to be practiced before it can be destroyed.

Although Mao Zedong was on the USSR payroll for many years, and he proclaimed "every member of our Chinese Communist Party is Stalin's pupil," he created his own style of Marxism-Leninism. He never renounced the Soviet version, saying he only changed it to meet the unique need of the Chinese people.

Principally, Mao believed the peasants could be the main force behind a revolution, but the proletariat and vanguard party still had to lead it. The resulting socialist government would first concentrate on rural, rather than industrial, development.

During a period of rectification between 1942 and 1944—as large numbers of new members entered the party—Mao created the basic methods of indoctrination and discipline that would rule the party for decades. An individual suspected of wrongful thinking was investigated, isolated, and required to engage in "thought examination," a written self-criticism of every private thought or action. Resistance or pleas of innocence were considered proof of deviance or treason.

Next, these individuals had to list everything suspicious or incorrect that others around them may have ever said or indicated by behavior.

Following their self criticism, people were brought before a small group of peers, who used what was learned to offer further criticism and verbal rebukes. The next step was to humiliate the person in a larger community meeting, which brought insults and public pressure to rehabilitate. When individuals were finally broken and confessed, they were forgiven and welcomed back into the group—where they were expected to spy on and denounce perceived deviance in other members.

Mao articulated his theory of the "Mass Line" in 1943, which purportedly established a way to consult the masses and allow them to participate in government, while at the same time asserting the necessity for central control of the masses.

Control ensured that everyone thought that Mao, alone, was the savior of the Chinese people. He perfected the ability to shift blame to others for failures and to take personal credit for every achievement. Badges with his image were worn by all top leaders, and millions of his portraits were printed and sold for private display.

The first use of the phrase "Mao Thought" resulted from an adoring article he caused to be written. The essence of Mao Thought is "seeking truth from facts." The Communist Party "must proceed from reality and put theory into practice in everything. In other words, the universal theory of Marxism-Leninism must be integrated with China's specific conditions."

Mao Thought has dominated China, its government, and its people for the past 70 years. Like Marxism, it's a little difficult to wrap one's mind around it; one can hear or read what the words say, but what do they mean? For an answer to that question, we must take a closer look at the reality of the person who spoke and wrote the words to determine the thinking, personality, and motivation behind his thoughts.

The Psychology of Mao

Mao Zedong's father, a wealthy peasant, was arbitrary and dictatorial in family matters—including the way he raised and educated his oldest surviving son, Mao.

After an arranged marriage, Mao's mother chose to live with her children in her family's nearby village. Mao loved his mother and hated his father. In later years, having the power to do so, he said he wished he could have had his father tortured.

As a child, Mao was spoiled by his mother and her family. He had light chores and learned to enjoy reading. Forced to return to his father's village at age eight, Mao began to study the Confucian classics and classical writing in a tutor's home to prepare for the imperial civil service examinations. Mao easily memorized the classics, but resisted academic and personal discipline by running away from or being expelled by a series of tutors. His father put him to work in the fields at age 13.

When he was 14, Mao entered an arranged marriage; however, his older wife died two years later. Learning there was a modern school in the area where his mother lived, Mao convinced his father to let him attend. For the first time, Mao was exposed to the world beyond China and its history and literature. After a few months, he transferred to a special school in the larger city of Changsha, the capital of Hunan province.

Life was good; Mao was seventeen years of age, and believed it had been easy for his father "to get rich." To use a baseball metaphor, Mao "was born on third base and thought he had hit a triple."

Mao arrived in Changsha in 1911, a year before the republican revolution broke out. He quickly became caught up in the revolution, cut off his own long-braided queue, and went about cutting off the pigtails of others. Mao joined a revolutionary army, but quit after a couple of months, as he did not like the military exercises or work. In what would become a pattern of his life, he hired someone else to perform his assigned water-carrying duties.

Mao tried another school, but left after six months and took up reading at a local library. Threatened by his father with a withdrawal of financial support, Mao entered a teacher's college at age 19. For the first time, he was exposed to Marxism and communism. He and a friend wandered the countryside, living by begging and writing decorative calligraphy for the peasants. Regarding this experience, Mao stated that people "worship hypocrisy, are content with being slaves, and [are] narrow-minded." He believed people were bored by peace and entertained by the drama of war and turmoil.

A few years later, when he was 24 years old, Mao wrote out a detailed personal philosophy similar to libertarian philosopher Ayn Rand's virtue of selfishness:

> I do not agree with the view that to be moral, the motive of one's action has to be benefitting others . . . . Of course, there are people and objects in the world, but they are all there only for me . . . . People like me only have a duty to ourselves; we have no duty to other people . . . . When Great Heroes give full play to their impulses, they are magnificently powerful, stormy, and invincible.

Mao was convinced he had a great role to play in changing China, saying it had to be destroyed and reformed, as must the rest of the world—indeed the entire universe. He wrote, "People like me long for its destruction, because when the old universe is destroyed, a new universe will be formed. Isn't that better?"

Following graduation, Mao borrowed money to travel to Beijing, where he stayed for six months working as a library assistant. The library was patronized by local intelligentsia, who snubbed Mao—giving rise to his lifetime resentment of intellectuals. Again borrowing money, Mao returned to Changsha, where he was employed as a part-time teacher in a primary school.

Mao wrote some early articles advocating the equality of women and their free choice in marriage, but he had no empathy for the burden of motherhood. He personally engaged in a lifetime of promiscuous affairs and was a serial adulterer during his many marriages.

With his first wife dead, and believing marriage was nothing but a "rape league," Mao never again entered into a formal marriage (or got a proper divorce). Contrary to Confucian principles of filial duty imbued in the Chinese culture, the manner in which Mao treated his wives and children are indicative of his character and provide an insight into his personality.

His second marriage to the daughter of one of his teachers forced her to accept a series of his extramarital affairs. She was to bear him three sons, two of whom lived. Mao abandoned this second wife when he left to hijack the Red Army. He acquired his third wife four months later.

The second wife was later executed by the Nationalists as a reprisal for Mao's actions, even though she had privately rejected him and his communist beliefs. There were repeated opportunities to rescue her, but Mao declined to go out of his way to do so. Raised by uncaring partisans, Mao's sons had no contact with their father, and they would often run away to live on the streets. Later, they were sent to study in Moscow and detained as hostages by Stalin.

When his third wife also attempted to reject Mao, he ordered guards to bring her with him "at all costs." She was forced to leave their first child, a daughter, with a wet nurse, and the child died before her mother could return for her. Their second child, a son, was abandoned when Mao and his third wife left on the Long March. The boy later disappeared and was never seen again.

Again pregnant, the third wife gave birth to a second baby girl during the march. This daughter was left with a peasant family and died several months later. After his wife was severely injured by an aerial bomb, Mao ordered she be carried on the march, although in her pain, she begged to be shot.

Once again pregnant, his wife left for Moscow to be treated for her injuries. She had to leave another child, a one-year-old daughter. In Moscow, she gave birth to a son, who died six months later. Mao did not respond when she wrote him about the death. She learned of his remarriage from a Russian newspaper article. When Mao did write, it was a one-sentence letter declaring their divorce. In later life, his third wife spent years, without success, searching for her abandoned children.

Mao's fourth wife was Jiang Qing, an actress from Shanghai, who came to Yan'an as a volunteer and appeared in shows. She herself had already been married and had relationships with a number of men. It was rumored she had sex with her jailers when she was imprisoned for being a communist. When Mao was criticized for this relationship, he arranged for his chief of security to say her past did not present a political problem.

Although Mao remained married to Jiang until his death, he shared his oversized bed with an endless series of attractive young women, sometimes alone and often with more than one. As he crudely told his doctor, "I wash my prick in their cunts." According to his personal physician, Mao went 25 years without taking a bath or brushing his teeth.

In George Orwell's classic *Animal Farm,* the Leader is a brutal pig protected by vicious dogs, who sleeps on a bed in the farmhouse. Because making decisions is so difficult, he gets milk in his mash and beer with his meals, while the other animals go hungry. The Leader is the only one who gets to service the sows. The ultimate Commandment of Animalism was "All animals are equal, but some animals are more equal than others." It is difficult to avoid making a comparison between Chairman Mao and Orwell's Leader.

Mao Establishes a Dynasty

It was in his exercise of violence and suffering that Mao demonstrated most clearly his lack of empathy or caring for other people. Early on during his supervision of the peasant associations in Hunan province for the Kuomintang, he supervised violence against landlords and others, Mao wrote how it produced "a kind of ecstasy never experienced before. It is wonderful!" Believing a "reign of terror in every county" was necessary, he gave his approval for people to be beaten to death, claiming it was no big deal.

If it gained him a benefit, Mao repeatedly caused his own troops to be slaughtered. There is no indication such deaths ever bothered Mao. Of the purges he implemented and supervised, the most egregious was the way he treated the youthful volunteers who came to Yan'an to join the communist cause.

Mao launched a spy hunt, suspecting the volunteers who defected from the Nationalists to be secret agents—in spite of his own early and exuberant involvement in the Kuomintang. More than 3,000 young people were imprisoned and many more placed under house arrest. Mao's detailed instructions for torture produced false confessions implicating others, who were then tortured. His own security detail estimated fewer than one percent were real spies, but Mao inflated that to ten percent. Even so, at least 2,700 fully innocent young people were tortured, which Mao compared to a father beating his sons, telling the victims not to bear him a grudge.

Wang Shiwei, a young journalist, published an article critical of institutional privileges in the Communist Party at Yan'an, saying those in power did not have "even elementary human sympathy!" The article cited differences in food and health care. When Wang put up a wall poster that said "Justice must be established in the Party. Injustice must be done away with," Mao accused him of being a Trotskyite and had him tortured and imprisoned until he recanted. Wang was later hacked to death.

What does all of this tell us about Mao? The standard psychiatric diagnosis of a psychopathic personality includes most of these factors: bold and uninhibited amoral and antisocial behavior, use of cruelty to gain power, lack of remorse or empathy, inability to love or establish meaningful personal relationships, and extreme egocentricity. A sadist is someone who finds pleasure, often sexual, by inflicting pain on others—someone who experiences *ecstasy* when imposing violence.

While some of these factors may be identified in successful corporate executives and winning political candidates, the question here is whether these behaviors have been exhibited by Mao Zedong thus far in this narrative? If so, what can we expect to find as we continue to review the essential history of China during his reign? Finally, what does the psychopathy and sadism of Mao portend for the present generation of Chinese young people who are told they must continue to be guided, as a matter of official government policy and constitutional law, by the thoughts of Mao?

The Communist Revolution

As the story of China and its people unfolds and we learn about the revolution that established the People's Republic of China, we have to consider both what happened and why it happened. The first question is easier to answer than the second.

The civil war really got going after General Marshall was unable to negotiate a unified government in February 1947, and it ended with the proclamation of the People's Republic of China in October 1949.

The Red Army evolved into the People's Liberation Army (PLA). The civil war was a brilliant victory by the communists and a stupid loss by Chiang Kai-shek—who insisted on personally commanding every failure. The overwhelming desire of the Chinese people for peace was a primary reason for the revolution's success. In addition to Chiang's inept leadership, the Nationalist's failure resulted from its ranks being thoroughly infiltrated by communist moles.

The USSR began a massive transfer of captured Japanese weapons and equipment to the PLA, including thousands of artillery pieces and hundreds of tanks. In addition, tens of thousands of Japanese prisoners were forced to secretly train the Liberation Army in the use of the seized equipment. Specifically, former Japanese pilots trained PLA pilots to fly the 900 Japanese aircraft transferred to the Chinese. Thousands of Japanese medical personnel established a system to treat sick and wounded PLA soldiers, instead of executing them, leaving them to die, or abandoning them to the care of peasants, as had been done in the past.

In payment for Soviet assistance, Mao shipped one million pounds of food each year to Russia. As a consequence, hundreds of thousands of Chinese people died of starvation in 1947 and 1948.

Chiang's first military mistake in the renewed civil war was his attempt to hold and govern the Manchurian cities, while the PLA occupied the surrounding countryside. The communists created an uprising of the peasantry by seizing and redistributing land from landlords and Japanese collaborators. Land reform programs were carried out with great violence. The Communist Party was able to infiltrate thousands of mind-programmed cadres into these areas to organize and impose discipline at a village level.

Mao believed his own son wasn't hard enough, and he ordered Mao An-Ying to participate in the atrocities and undergo self-criticism. When the level of violence associated with land reform became so great as to threaten success of the revolution, Mao ordered another top official to take the blame and to write a self-criticism absolving Mao of responsibility.

The best military decision Mao ever made was placing Lin Biao in command of the Liberation Army. Lin had been with Mao since the Jiangxi Soviet and participated in the Long March. As one of the most able communist officers, Chiang Kai-shek offered a $100,000 reward for Lin's head.

Whenever the Nationalist Army ventured out of the cities, it was drawn further into the countryside, harassed by lightning attacks, surrounded, and destroyed. Its American-made equipment was seized; its officers were killed, and its soldiers were recruited into the Liberation Army.

As the Nationalist forces in the cities became weaker, the PLA grew to more than 1,500,000 troops, who were well-armed with captured

Japanese and American equipment. Lin Biao began to pick off the cities, one by one, until all of Manchuria was captured by the end of 1948. In one city—which the Nationalist Army refused to surrender—Mao did not allow any civilians to leave, causing the deaths of more than 120,000 Chinese people during the siege.

Making use of its extraordinary discipline, the Communist Party effectively administered the northern cities. The streets were clean, crime was suppressed, labor unions were formed, and the wages of workers increased. In contrast, the Nationalist government (and Chiang's own family) was riddled with corruption. It laid heavy taxes on the people and failed to control the economy, as inflation soared. The government also came down hard on the student peace movement, believing it to be a communist conspiracy.

Turning south after the fall of Manchuria, Lin Biao captured Tianjin in January 1949.

As the Liberation Army continued its advance, Chiang concentrated his Nationalist Army at Huai-Hai in an attempt to block the path to Nanjing and the Yangtze river. In the largest set battle of the civil war, Chiang's plans were revealed by a communist mole, who was also in a position to advise and mislead Chiang—as he personally directed the losing battle.

The Nationalist armored force of tanks, which Chiang held in reserve, could not be deployed because it was encircled with tank traps dug by millions of peasants under Deng Xiaoping's command. The 300,000 man Nationalist Army was surrounded and forced to surrender.

With the capture of Huai-Hai, the communists seized control of China north of the Yangtze River. As the Nationalist Army continued to disintegrate, the Liberation Army quickly captured Nanjing in April and Shanghai in May.

Rather than surrender, Chiang Kai-shek and two million of his military and political supporters fled to Taiwan in December 1949, taking with him China's financial and art treasures. The Nationalist troops left behind either surrendered or escaped into Burma and other southern countries.

In the meantime, Mao moved into the Zhongnanhai compound—a vast imperial leisure garden located adjacent to the Forbidden City in Beijing. The garden was started by the Jin dynasty, completed by the Ming dynasty, and renovated by the Qing dynasty. Surrounded by high walls, the garden is laid out with villas built in the parkland around two huge lakes and is equipped with waterfalls and pavilions. Like the Leader's farmhouse in *Animal Farm*, the garden became the residential compound of Mao and the first rulers of Communist dynasty. It remains the administrative center of those who presently rule China, including the Communist Party Central Committee and State Council.

Establishing the People's Republic of China

On October 1, 1949, Mao stood atop the Tiananmen Gate in Beijing and declared the existence of the People's Republic of China. Other communist leaders stood near, including Zhou Enlai and Deng Xiaoping. One hundred thousand people cheered "Long live Chairman Mao." His rule would last, unchallenged, for 27 more years until his death in 1976. His power of life and death over the half billion Chinese people—like the dynastic emperors of old—was absolute.

Mao modeled the Chinese government on the USSR, with some differences. It primarily consists of the State Council, which is chaired by the Premier (prime minister) and includes the vice premiers and the ministers of the major departments. The Council meets every six months. When it is not in session, the government is controlled by the Politburo, which meets weekly or during emergencies. On a daily basis, the government is managed by a Standing Committee of the Politburo that includes the Premier, an executive vice premier, three vice premiers, and five other state councilors.

The State Council is one of three interlocking branches of government, the other two being the Chinese Communist Party and the People's Liberation Army. The Council is primarily concerned with administering both the central government and the provinces, and each vice premier has assigned areas of administrative responsibility.

Unlike the Soviet system in which the Communist Party controlled the government, in China the leading members of the three branches are all one and the same. For example, although there is a Ministry of Defense, the Army is listed in the government organization chart as being under the Central Military Commission, which in turn is supervised by the Standing Committee of the National People's Congress. On paper, this Commission is represented as the commander-in-chief of the armed forces. As a matter-of-fact, the Army is actually under the command of the identically named Central Military Commission of the Communist Party. The two commissions have identical memberships.

The Chinese Communist Party has ruled the People's Republic of China ever since it was proclaimed by Mao in 1949. Purportedly, the highest authority of the Party is its National Congress, which meets every five years. In practice, most decisions are made in advance by Party leaders. Between congresses, the Communist Party is governed by the Central Committee, which meets once a year. When it is not in session, and on a daily basis, the Party is governed by the Politburo and its Standing Committee.

The leader of the Communist Party is its General Secretary, who can also be the Chairman of the Central Military Commission and the state President. When all three of these offices are held by the same person, he is known as the "paramount leader." Xi Jinping, who was elected President at the 18th National Congress in 2012 is the current paramount leader, and all three branches of the government are under his control.

There are no other real political parties in China, even though the Communist Party is nominally a part of the United Front, which consists of eight other legally authorized "parties." The Front has representation in the National People's Congress; however, it is totally controlled by the Communist Party.

The National People's Congress (different from the Party Congresses that meet every five years) is the legislative body of China and, under the

Chinese constitution, is the top state power in the government; however, its almost 3,000 members vote as directed by the Communist Party. One reason for this is that all of the delegates are disciplined members of the Party, which selects those who attend.

Clearly, the People's Republic of China is not a government of or by the Chinese people, nor is it a republic. By name, the People's Republic should belong to the people of China. In fact the Republic's government is a Marxist-Leninist dictatorship of, by, and for the Chinese Communist Party and its members—as was intended by Mao.

Mao's Insane Reign

Several different times China made great strides forward during the reign of Mao Zedong, and several times Mao destroyed much of each success in order to confirm his belief in "permanent revolution." Mao stated, "In making revolution, one must strike while the iron is hot—one revolution must follow another, the revolution must continually advance."

Unlike the emperors of old, Mao's primary purpose was not to care for the people of his empire, but to make China so powerful he could "Control the Earth."

Communist control of China was secured with much violence. Almost immediately there was a campaign to suppress counter-revolutionaries, during which Mao insisted on "massive arrests" and "massive killings." He was "very delighted," when his chastisement of a provincial cadre for not killing enough people resulted in an increase. He wanted maximum exposure to killings—in Beijing alone, 30,000 public sentencing and execution rallies were held. Altogether, three million people died during his land reform program.

Mao launched an anti-corruption campaign in which he called for thousands to be executed as a deterrent against embezzlement. At the same time, he constructed more than 50 mansions throughout China in every province, many with swimming pools, for his exclusive use should he deign to visit.

While imposing strict puritanical standards on the people of China, Mao enjoyed the sexual services of an unlimited supply of young women from the Army's entertainment troupes. The Army called the procurement process "selecting imperial concubines."

Taking Control of the Nation

The People's Republic of China was able to take administrative control fairly quickly by retaining two million of the remaining Kuomintang officials, until Party cadres could learn to perform their jobs. The borders were expanded and secured by the "liberation" of Tibet and reincorporation of Manchuria.

A People's Political Consultative Conference adopted an Organic Law, which rubber-stamped a "democratic dictatorship," led by the Communist Party, to govern China. The Conference also adopted a Common Program establishing equality for women and minorities, continuing land redistribution to peasants, and the development of heavy industry. The program provided for the freedoms of thought, speech, publication, assembly, association, correspondence, and movement. Of course, "Political reactionaries" were an exception—those who failed to share Mao's opinion had no rights.

Inflation was brought under control by seizing banks, establishing commodity trading associations, and by paying salaries in commodities, such as grain, cloth, or oil.

Mao traveled to Moscow in 1949 and negotiated a Sino-Soviet Treaty of Alliance and Mutual Assistance with Stalin. Manchuria and Xinjiang were designated as Soviet spheres of influence—allowing Russian access to their mineral resources. The treaty also extended a $300 million line of credit to China, primarily for the purchase of military equipment.

Repayment came due the next year when Stalin authorized North Korea to invade the South, with the understanding China would step in if needed. When the United Nations forces, primarily composed of U.S. troops, defeated the North Koreans and advanced toward the Yalu River and the border of China, Mao responded.

As many as 3,000,000 Chinese troops ultimately crossed the river and, using human wave tactics, drove the U.N. forces back down the Korean peninsula to the 38th parallel—where a truce was finally negotiated in 1953. More than 400,000 Chinese troops, including Mao's eldest son, died in the war. Mao showed no sign of grief and did not inform his daughter-in-law of her husband's death for more than two years.

China became deeply indebted to Russia, as it acknowledged the urgent need to modernize its military to fight the new Cold War. Nonetheless, the Soviets did not give anything to China for free—every bullet and machine had to be paid for by scarce agricultural products. Payment was literally taken from the mouths of the Chinese people. Mao dismissed the hunger of his people with comments such as, "Having only tree leaves to eat? So be it."

Under the Agrarian Reform Law of 1950, land reform was extended throughout China. By 1952, the program was largely completed, benefiting 60 percent of the peasants. Land seizure was accomplished by great violence and terror, resulting in the deaths of millions of landlords and rich peasants. Under redistribution, each peasant received approximately a fourth of an acre, and grain production rose more than 12 percent in the first two years.

Just as the Nationalist bureaucracy was left intact, the basic economy of Chinese businesses and industry was initially left alone, except for that which had been operated by the Kuomintang or abandoned by the fleeing Nationalists. These were immediately seized, and as many as 200,000 professionals were left in place to operate them.

Due to the shortage of management personnel when the communists took control of the government and economy, untested cadres were incorporated into the Party. In 1951, using the Korean War as an excuse, Mao launched another campaign against counter-revolutionaries. Using the tools of denunciation and self-criticism he had perfected earlier, ten percent of all Party cadres were eliminated and between a half million and 800,000 Party members were killed.

Following the Soviet model, Mao announced his first Five-year Plan in 1953. It sought to introduce central planning, transfer the ownership of all private property to state control, increase heavy industry, and collectivize agriculture. The peasants—who earlier had land distributed to them—were now forced to surrender their land, implements, and livestock to local collectives.

Stalin helped China by extending credit for the purchase of manufacturing equipment. In one of the greatest technological transfers in history, Russia provided seven iron and steel plants, 24 power stations and 63 machinery plants, along with more than a hundred other major projects. To assemble and operate the plants, Stalin allowed the employment of 11,000 Soviet technicians and trained 28,000 Chinese students in Russia. Subject to the requirements of central planning, these enterprises were operated under the Russian system of authoritarian "one-man management." Overall, the effort resulted in a doubling of industrial output, particularly in steel, oil and chemicals.

While agriculture production had shown significant increases under private ownership, Mao came to believe rural initiative presented a capitalist threat. In addition, he wanted to derive more state income from agriculture to support his efforts to increase heavy industry. Mao ordered agriculture to be further organized using the Soviet model and for individual farmers to be herded into local producers' cooperatives. These were further concentrated into Advanced Producers' Cooperatives. At this stage, individual peasants lost all title to their land. Based on their labor, they received a salary, paid in agricultural products.

Collectivization was largely completed by 1956. The net result was to place individual farmers under six layers of government and Communist Party administration that reached directly into every household. The grain monopoly controlled all elements of production, pricing, purchase, and distribution.

In exchange for their labor, and to receive a distribution of food, farmers had to show their certificate of household registration. This requirement tied them to the land, and much like serfs, they could not obtain food if they tried to relocate or travel. As Party members, local cadres and higher echelon leaders gained extraordinary power and many were corrupted.

To obtain the agricultural products he needed for foreign exchange, Mao imposed starvation conditions on the Chinese people—allowing them only 190 kilos of processed grain each per year. He ordered:

"Educate peasants to eat less, and have more thin gruel." Responding to questions of conscience, he said, "Some of our comrades have too much mercy, not enough brutality, which means they are not so Marxist."

Modeled on Stalin's 1936 Soviet constitution, Mao promulgated a constitution for the People's Republic of China in 1954 to replace the Common Program. The result was to coordinate the government and Communist Party administrations with dual memberships, as earlier discussed. Power remained concentrated in the Standing Committee of the Politburo of the Central Committee, which was chaired by Mao.

In balancing the essential need for education to operate a modern economy, with the need of his dictatorship to retain total control, Mao set out to reeducate teachers and professors about Marxism-Leninism. These professionals had to undergo the same process of self-criticism and denunciation Mao had earlier put his first young volunteers through. They had to confess their guilt for betraying the people by serving capitalistic masters and exhibit their gratitude to Chairman Mao for leading them on the correct path.

Using the Soviet model, Mao reformed the Chinese education system by destroying liberal arts education and supplementing it with polytechnic and engineering colleges and universities. Out of the 200 remaining schools of higher education, he allowed only 13 to offer both arts and sciences. Russian texts were adopted, and Russian, rather than English, became the required second language of students.

Deng Xiaoping, who was serving as General Secretary, believed it was possible for intellectuals to join farmers and workers as members of the Party. He also believed it was essential to encourage and support non-party intellectuals—if the larger goals of the Communist Party were to be achieved.

The Hundred Flowers Campaign (1956-1957)

In a cynical ruse to flush out dissent, Mao stated in 1956, "The policy of letting a hundred flowers bloom and a hundred schools of thought contend is designed to promote the flourishing of the arts and the progress of science." In private, he said he was "casting a long line to bait big fish."

Intellectuals were encouraged to criticize communist cadres and to express an opinion about Party practices. These criticisms were to be constructive and consistent with loyalty to the communist system. Little was said for a year, but in 1957, intellectuals began to openly speak out about the foundation of the Communist Party, its policies, doctrines, and methods. The competence of cadres was criticized for interfering with scientific research. Students from Beijing University used the adjoining Democracy Wall to paste up posters critical of officials. One compared the Party to Hitler stating, "Totalitarian power is peril!"

The program was quickly shut down, and the shears were unsheathed. Critics were forced to self-criticize and to denounce others who had engaged in wrongful thinking.

In what became known as the Anti-Rightist Campaign of 1957-1958, Mao accused the intellectuals of being rightists. Deng Xiaoping chopped the flowers by firing as many as 700,000 educated and highly-skilled people—many of whom had actively supported the revolution and believed in its published principles. Mao informed the leadership that in just one province, Hunan, 100,000 were denounced, 10,000 were arrested, and 1,000 were killed. He said, "The other provinces did the same. So our problems were solved."

The campaign empowered and promoted economic and cultural fundamentalists—who were ignorant about the world outside of China—into the leadership class. It severed the nation's intellectual resources just when they were most needed, and the Chinese people suffered from this massacre of informed reason for decades.

Mao believed the intellectuals did not have a correct revolutionary consciousness, and he rejected their contributions to economic development. From this point forward, intellectuals were hated and persecuted, as being too smart for Mao Thought.

The Great Leap Forward (1958-1961)

Although the first Five-Year Plan produced a significant improvement in industrial output, Mao began charting a new course. He replaced the Soviet one-man rule of industry with collective leadership under Party control, and he de-emphasized heavy industry in favor of agriculture and the development of light industry.

The change from Soviet-style management coincided with Mao's breakup with the USSR after Khrushchev denounced Stalin in 1956. Khrushchev denied the inevitability of war with the capitalist nations. Mao disagreed and believed Khrushchev was harming the drive for international communism.

The final blow to Sino-Soviet relations came in June 1959, when Khrushchev stopped assisting China's development of nuclear weapons. Khrushchev believed Mao "was bursting with an impatient desire to rule the world." Mao had been counting on the atomic bomb to avoid having to modernize the Liberation Army—which relied on massive infantry, human-wave tactics, and guerrilla warfare. Enough was learned from the Russian scientists to allow China to move forward on the bomb, which was first tested in 1964.

Knowing atom bombs would be soon available, Mao wanted to quickly obtain the missiles and ships to deliver them. He was impatient to conquer the world. In August 1958, Mao told a group of provincial leaders, "In the future we will set up the Earth Control Committee, and make a uniform plan for the Earth." In speaking to army officers, he said, "Now the Pacific Ocean is not peaceful. It can only be peaceful when we take it over."

In preparation, Mao and other Party leaders came to realize the Soviet model did not answer all of China's needs. The collectivization of agriculture had not produced the expected gains. Continuing to repay the Soviet loans with agricultural products, China was unable to feed its growing population.

In what became known as the Great Leap Forward, Mao declared in January 1958 that "it is possible to catch up with Britain in 15 years." His slogan became "More, better, faster, cheaper," and production quotas for industry and agriculture were increased to impossible levels.

Using the physical labor of 100 million peasants, large-scale projects were undertaken, including an immense program of rural irrigation. To better mobilize the massive labor forces required for these projects, the Agricultural Producers' Cooperatives were abolished and consolidated into larger People's Communes. Collective kitchens and nurseries were established to allow greater numbers of women to participate in the forced labor. Massed labor toiled on major projects, such as dams and rural industries, including "backyard steel furnaces." Wildly exorbitant production schedules were promulgated and the number of workers in state-owned industries doubled.

Estimated costs of projects calculated the number of expected deaths per cubic meter of earth moved—30 billion cubic meters would result in the deaths of 30,000 workers. Local officials who complained were accused of being a "Rightist anti-Party clique." Much of the work was abandoned before completion, or it quickly failed. One series of reservoirs collapsed during a storm in 1975, killing almost a quarter million people.

There was a vast expansion of agricultural schools, where students were required to provide productive labor. Peasants were organized into militias and armed to participate in the expected liberation of Taiwan.

Disillusionment quickly set in when it was realized that cadres had responded to the wildly exorbitant production schedules with wildly deceptive and equally exorbitant production reports. Faced with internal political resistance, Mao resigned as President of the People's Republic in December 1958, although he retained power as the Chairman of the Communist Party. Liu Shaoqi, Mao's designated successor, was appointed President.

Seven months later, in July 1959, Mao received a letter from the Minister of Defense, Peng Dehuai. An early supporter, Peng was a survivor of the Long March and Mao's top general in the Korean War. Peng privately warned Mao the reported production statistics of the Great Leap Forward were being greatly exaggerated and the effects were having a devastating impact on the peasantry. Instead of listening to his old comrade, Mao took the criticism personally and attacked Peng for leading an "anti-Party clique." Peng was replaced as Minister of Defense by Lin Biao, the general who had commanded the revolution.

Fearing opposition, Mao convened a non-voting Conference of the Seven Thousand in January 1962. In his own address, Mao claimed "our domestic situation is on the whole good," and announced plans for another great leap forward. To his surprise and great anger, President Liu Shaoqi delivered a speech different from the written one he had submitted. Liu told the truth about the agricultural failures saying there "is not only no Great Leap Forward, but a great deal of falling backward." Liu had the support of the delegates, as Mao blamed others for the famine.

Finally conceding their stumbles, the Great Leaps were abandoned. It took years for their consequences to become fully known, and they were devastating. Rather than an increase, food production declined at the same time food was being shipped to the USSR as debt payment. In addition, the food distribution system of the Agricultural Producers' Cooperatives was destroyed by the new People's Communes. The result was one of the greatest famines in human history, the full extent of which may never be known.

Demographic studies have shown there to have been at least 16 to 27 million deaths from starvation and illnesses exacerbated by starvation. Other estimates run as high as 38 million. Even before the famine ended, Liu Shaoqi confirmed the deaths of 30 million. At the same time, grain exports sufficient to feed all of these people continued to be shipped to the Soviet Union.

China's emperors believed it was a part of their familial duty to construct and fill granaries to feed their people during droughts and bad times. To the contrary, Mao could not have cared less. "Half of China may well have to die," he said. Mao claimed he was "prepared to sacrifice 300 million Chinese for the victory of world revolution."

While the truth may have been concealed from the Chinese people and the outside world, the Party leadership was aware of the full extent of the disaster, and voices other than Mao's were being listened to.

Deng Xiaoping and Liu Shaoqu were among the moderates who gained influence in the Communist Party. They sought accurate and factual reports to document the true situation of the economy, and discovered there had been a mass unsustainable migration to the cities. Many of the overly ambitious plants had to be closed, resulting in a 50 percent reduction in urban job opportunities. To avoid having to feed the unemployed, up to 30 million workers were shipped back to the countryside, and illegal internal migration was curtailed.

The Great Proletarian Cultural Revolution (1966-1976)

Differences between moderates and conservatives began to intensify. Expert economic planners predicted that return to the cultivation of privately controlled plots would provide greater production, which could be distributed through local markets. Mao opposed this concept of "individual responsibility," and called instead for a renewal of the class struggle. The moderates prevailed and a plan for "agriculture first" was developed.

Investments were made in fertilizer and equipment, and individuals were allowed to lease plots of land on the local level. By 1965, output of agricultural products reached the level it had been in 1957—although there were 80 million more people to feed. Industrial development also proceeded, even though technological resources were diverted for the development of the atomic bomb and other military schemes.

While still holding the levers of power, Mao's influence had declined and he had less to do with the day-to-day operation of the government. His wife, former actress Jiang Qing, remained active in cultural affairs and was the head of the Army's Cultural Department.

The constitution was amended to delete Mao Thought as the leading principle and to allow white-collar workers into the Party. Technocrats began to have more power and were appointed to the Politburo. At the same time, steps were taken to rectify issues between the bureaucracy and the people. Mao was not satisfied with these steps, and he complained about the correct way to handle the contradictions.

The primary problem was apathy and corruption among Party cadres at the local level, which everyone agreed was serious. Mao proposed that cadres be investigated by local peasant associations, while the moderates, including Deng and Liu, wanted to deploy urban-based work teams to carry out rectification.

Mao castigated the bureaucrats for their arrogance and concluded that contradictions between the Party and the people had become antagonistic and beyond rectification. Saying the Party was unable to correct itself, Mao began to attack his own creation.

In 1965, Mao issued a document which made it clear his target was not local cadres, but the party leadership itself, which he accused of taking the capitalist road. This was the commencement of a purge Mao had been planning against those who had earlier defied him—especially President Liu Shaoqi.

Mao claimed that revolutionary concern for the class of ordinary people and their collectives was being revised in favor of a ruling class of party leaders, intellectuals, and other specially-privileged and urbanized interests. This elite bureaucracy was exploiting the peasant masses. Mao defined revisionism as an abandonment of the revolutionary goals by the elite, who were living a capitalistic lifestyle. This from the man with 50 mansions and a limitless cadre of mistresses.

Mao turned to the People's Liberation Army and Lin Biao, whom he had installed as the Minister of Defense following Peng Dehua's defiance during the Great Leap Forward debate. Lin wholeheartedly supported Mao and ordered the printing of the *Quotations from Chairman Mao Zedong* (The Little Red Book), which was widely distributed in the army. He praised Mao's leadership during the war against Japan, which, he claimed, was fought with masses of soldiers instead of machines.

Public education, which had been rolled back following the Great Leap Forward, also became a matter of concern for Mao and the conservatives. In particular, Mao's call for a continuing class struggle was not being served by the two-track education system. The system provided a higher quality education in the urban areas, particularly to the children of the Party cadres. Mao believed teachers and testing held too much power, and education should be more practically evaluated by its effect on production. In January 1965, Mao lectured the Politburo, urging it to implement a Cultural Revolution in China.

Culture was the issue that brought matters to a head. Mao had always argued that art should serve the revolution and proletariat goals, and not be critical of political issues. An opera about an upright official being dismissed by a corrupt Ming emperor was interpreted by the public as criticizing Mao's actions during the Great Leap Forward. Displeased, he asked his wife, Jiang Qing, to formulate a policy on cultural matters. Mao once said "Jiang Qing is as deadly poisonous as a scorpion," and she set about to prove him right. She gathered a team, which came to be called the Gang of Four. They began to present a radical viewpoint and denounced all forms of culture as being opposed to Mao Thought.

Lin Biao had been engaged in policy differences with his own army Chief of Staff, and Lin accused his Chief and others of plotting a coup. The charge was made at a meeting of the Politburo in May 1966 and resulted in a circular, alleging the Party had been infiltrated by bourgeois revisionists. This circular launched the Cultural Revolution against revisionists in order to restore Mao's original revolutionary principles.

Mao truly believed continual revolution was the correct path to communism, irrespective of consequences, and he believed spiritual regeneration should take precedence over economic development.

A Central Cultural Revolution Group, consisting of Jiang Qing and other radicals, replaced the Central Committee Secretariat and was made directly responsible to the Standing Committee of the Politburo.

Although he was its principal target, President Liu Shaoqi was placed in nominal charge of the Cultural Revolution. Liu was quickly undermined by Mao—who encouraged radicals in the universities to oppose party leaders and their own school administrators. Posters attacking educational policies and leaders began to appear, and Mao broadcast their contents.

Mao's Insane Reign

Liu dispatched work teams to the universities to rectify issues and assert the Party's authority, but his efforts were opposed by the radicals. Mao accused Liu's teams of "adopting the reactionary stand of the bourgeoisie."

Divisions within the movement were between those who came from "bourgeois," or intellectual backgrounds, and those with "red" backgrounds, including peasants, workers, soldiers, and Party cadres. The bourgeois students had enjoyed the better educational track and supported Liu's rectification teams, while the red students began to directly challenge the teams.

The Cultural Revolution was formalized by the publication of "Sixteen Points" by the Party Central Committee, which called for the Revolution "to struggle against and overthrow those persons in authority who are taking the capitalist road, to criticize and repudiate the reactionary bourgeois academic 'authorities' and the ideology of the bourgeoisie."

Mao endorsed the name of Red Guards for the student radicals, who were plastering big posters on campuses. He issued his own poster calling for students to "Bombard the Headquarters." Red Guards began to assemble on most campuses, and Mao reviewed their massive rallies in Tiananmen Square.

Wearing his army uniform, Mao spoke to a rally of Red Guards and told them to "learn revolution by making revolution" throughout the country. Lin Biao urged the destruction of old ideas, culture, customs, and habits. The Red Guards relied on these instructions to destroy art and anything that appeared foreign—including clothing and hairstyles.

Students attacked their own administrators and teachers. Red Guards attacked rural Party officials and invaded factories and communes to destroy the Party's authority over workers and peasants. With army assistance, the Red Guards took control of government offices and factories.

Virtually every home in China was invaded. Everything of value was seized for the regime, and all objects of culture, including books, were destroyed. At the specific direction of the Gang of Four, the home of Confucius was wrecked.

As the reign of terror began to spin out of control, Mao and the Cultural Revolution Group urged the creation of revolutionary committees—combining representatives of the mass groups, Party cadres, and the army.

Red Guard units were being armed, and fighting was breaking out. China was at the brink of total civil war: Jiang Qing's criticisms of the army undermined its authority; the foreign ministry was seized by the Guards; the Soviet and Indonesian legations were invaded; and the British embassy was burned to the ground.

Encouraged by Lin Biao and Zhou Enlai, Mao began to rein in the Cultural Revolution. Some radicals were purged, and the army was ordered to quell civil disorders.

Early in 1968, the Red Guards were demobilized in favor of an accelerated formation of revolutionary committees. The first stage of the Cultural Revolution was concluded, but it was far from over.

Mao deployed an adult group of Red Rebels to purge the top leaders he had targeted all along. Many were tortured to death in public displays, which were photographed. Hundreds of thousands, if not millions of former officials were sent to labor camps. In these camps could also be found exiled artists, writers, and composers.

Some of the worse persecution was reserved for President Liu Shaoqi and his wife, who were terrorized, beaten, and held in solitary confinement. Both refused to admit uncommitted crimes. Liu was declared to be the "commander of China's bourgeoisie headquarters." He was confined in his home and slowly starved to death, as he became increasingly confused and debilitated from diabetes. He was kept alive long enough to be removed as President and purged from the Party at a Congress in April 1959. He died a month later, but his death was not revealed for 12 years, until after Mao died. His wife, accused of being an American spy, was imprisoned until Mao's death. Their children were beaten and thrown in the street. One son committed suicide.

Lin Biao was designated as Mao's successor. He was not appointed to replace Liu as President, and the position remained vacant.

Mao's Insane Reign

The radical Cultural Revolution Group forced Deng Xiaoping to make a self-criticism, and he was kept under house arrest for two years. In 1969, he was sent to work in a tractor factory in Jiangxi province. Deng's son was tortured and fell from a high window of his college dormitory. Initially refused medical treatment because Deng was under criticism, his son was rendered a paraplegic.

Deng spent the four years of his exile considering how to preserve the Party's role of providing correct leadership. He thought about how to reconcile Party leadership with the massive errors committed by Mao, and to learn from those mistakes in creating more practical social and economic policies.

Mao's influence over the future course of China was guaranteed at the Ninth Party Congress in 1969, when a new constitution reemphasized the ideologies of Mao Thought and class struggle. Two-thirds of the 1,500 attendees wore military uniforms, and 45 percent of the new Central Committee were members of the army.

While the economy began to recover, managers remained fearful of political reprisal and had to work with army-dominated revolutionary committees.

The Revolution had both a positive and negative effect on education. On the one hand, primary school enrollment rose by 50 percent, the number of secondary students increased from 20 million to 67 million, and a redistribution of resources benefitted rural students. On the other hand, the quality of higher education was greatly diminished.

Post-secondary education in colleges and universities did not resume until the early 1970s, and entrance testing was replaced by recommendations from revolutionary committees. One of the great ironies of the Cultural Revolution was the dispatch of four million former Red Guard student members to the countryside for up to ten years—which precluded higher education for most.

Although Mao had used Lin Biao and the army to regain his power in the party and government, he began to have differences with Lin about foreign policy, including relations with the United States. Lin's efforts to be officially designated as Mao's successor were rebuffed, and Mao began to talk about Lin behind his back with regional military commanders.

Lin Biao's son, with his knowledge, began to conspire to assassinate Mao. When the plans were discovered by Zhou Enlai, Lin Biao attempted to escape with his wife and son to the Soviet Union. Their air force plane crashed in Mongolia in 1976.

With Lin out of the way, the primary question was who would replace him as Mao's designated successor. Would it be one of the radical faction or the more moderate group headed by Zhou Enlai? After considering several dark horses, Mao turned to Deng Xiaoping, whom he had earlier accused of having traveled the "capitalist road." Deng was not alone in being forgiven, Mao agreed to rehabilitate 400 other former senior Party officials. Starting with this small leadership group, Zhou and Deng were able to save the Party and China.

Although the Cultural Revolution had not yet reached the end of its destructive path, 60 percent of Party officials had already been purged from office. There were untold millions of victims; at least 400,000—some say three million—died directly or as the result of torture and maltreatment.

Deng Xiaoping Takes Charge

Deng returned to Beijing in 1973 and was slowly given party responsibilities. Restored as a member of the Central Committee, he had the power to reduce the size of the bloated army and to promulgate an economic plan prepared by Zhou Enlai. Known as the "Four Modernizations," these included science and technology, defense, industry, and agriculture. Deng's authority increased when Mao concluded Zhou was too soft toward the United States during his negotiations with Henry Kissinger, U.S. President Nixon's National Security Advisor. Deng was made a full member of the Politburo and Central Military Commission.

In 1974, Mao assigned Deng to deliver China's presentation to the United Nations General Assembly. The speech divided the economic development of nations into the first, second and third worlds. In a side meeting with Kissinger, Deng stressed domestic relations with the United States. Deng visited Wall Street and bought some toys for his grandchildren.

Mao appointed Deng first vice premier of the State Council. Combined with his other assignments, the position gave him the power to guide the economy. Rather than confrontational rectification, Deng relied on consolidation to identify key individuals and form teams to attack the most serious issues. Using this approach, he was able to consolidate and solve military, railroad, coal, and steel problems.

Deng emphasized science and technology above the other modernizations and revived the Chinese Academy of Sciences. It was combined with the Academy of Social Sciences allowing the first tentative steps toward the study of philosophy, and beginning work in culture and the arts was allowed.

Deng continued to be dogged by the radicals, particularly Jiang Qing. Mao became concerned Deng was moving too fast, failing to support the Cultural Revolution and neglecting class struggle. When Zhou Enlai died in January 1976—after Mao intentionally delayed his surgery for recurring bladder cancer—Mao did not advance Deng to be Premier. Instead, Mao reaffirmed the Cultural Revolution and appointed Hua Guofeng, a nondescript supporter of the Revolution.

Contrary to the wishes of the Gang of Four—who banned any mourning—two million people lined up to watch the passing of Zhou's hearse and funeral procession. A similar number engaged in spontaneous demonstrations in Tiananmen Square. Believing Deng, who had read Zhou's eulogy, had something to do with the event, the Gang used force to break up the "counter-revolutionary" demonstration. Commending the violent suppression, Mao wrote "Great Morale-booster. Good. Good. Good."

Deng was placed under detention in Beijing and later released to house arrest. He was once again out of power, but only for one year. When a massive earthquake 160 miles southeast of Beijing, killed 242,000 people and damaged one-third of the buildings in Beijing, the Gang incongruously encouraged survivors to increase their criticism of Deng Xiaoping.

The Death of Mao

The earthquake and the Gang's cynical response to it may have been the last straw. As in the days of emperor rule, when such natural disasters often portended the end of a dynasty, Mao died two months later in September 1976. Nearly blind and suffering the final paralysis of amyotrophic lateral sclerosis (Lou Gehrig's disease), Mao spend his last days cursing his old enemies. He expressed no remorse for the 70 million Chinese people who died as a result of his insane rule. Deng was not allowed to pay his last respects.

Mao outlasted his old enemy, Chiang Kai-shek, by one year. Both led one-party dictatorships to the ends of their lives. Chiang was survived by his son, who went on to create a freely elected representative government in Taiwan. Mao's legacy of a dictatorial communist dynasty continues to this day. His massive portrait still dominates Tiananmen Square, and Mao Thought continues to guide the Chinese Communist Party and its domain—the People's Republic of China.

Deng's Moderate Rule

The nation Mao bequeathed to his heirs was in chaos. Its people were destitute, with most of those who were not members of the Communist Party living in dire poverty. For decades, government spending had been concentrated on the military and arms-related industries, with little left for water, sewage, electricity, and housing. There were shortages of all necessities, including food, clothing, education, and health care. The Chinese people had neither bread, nor circuses, as everything entertaining and the least bit cultural was banned.

Mao's memorial service was held in September 1976, and his widow stood next to Hua Guofeng on the gate of Tiananmen Square as he read the eulogy. Rather than playing their expected leading role in the following act, Hua ordered the arrest of Jiang and other Gang members. Charged with plotting to usurp power, they were held in custody for four years until receiving life sentences. Jiang committed suicide in 1991. During their trials, the government presented evidence the Gang had falsely accused and persecuted more than 700,000 people, of whom 35,000 had died. Everyone was aware the number of victims far exceeded these allegations, but China had to move on.

Hua remained Premier and became Chairman of the Party and Central Military Commission. Although he allowed the criticism of Deng to continue, radical Maoism was coming to an end. Hua delayed Deng's return to power, but he did not reverse the economic progress Deng had started.

Within a year, the criticism of Deng tapered off and senior Party leaders, particularly those who held power before the Cultural Revolution, began to debate when Deng should be brought back to work and what position he should hold. After Deng wrote a letter confirming his support of Hua, he resumed the posts he previously held. He became First Vice Premier in July 1977 and the Chair of the Party National Committee in March 1978.

Deng's primary assignment was to manage science, technology, and education. He encouraged senior Party officials to travel overseas and see firsthand what the United States and other countries were doing and how their people lived. One high-level group briefed the Politburo on its return, and the State Council convened a special forum to consider how best to take advantage of Western technology and capital. Instructions were to plan what China should do in the future. The essential conclusion was that China should open up its economy to foreign trade and capital.

The strategy to achieve modernization defined by Deng required China to have an economic structure that rewarded those who advanced science, technology, and productivity. Deng advocated individual responsibility, with commensurate authority and accountability. He said, "It doesn't matter whether the cat is black or the cat is white. What matters is that it catches mice."

Deng, who had studied in Paris as a youth, encouraged young people to study abroad and experience foreign life. Initially thousands, and then more than a million students left the country to study overseas between 1978 and 2007. Many returned to participate in and lead the development of business, science, and technology.

By the end of 1978, the support and consensus of the senior Party leadership made Deng the Paramount Leader of China above Hua, who remained as Premier until he resigned in 1980. Hua continued to chair the Party's Central Military Commission for another year, when Deng took over the powerful chairs of the Military Commission and Central Advisory Commission.

Deng's moderate rule allowed China to recover from Mao's deprecations. Nonetheless, he remained a committed Marxist and believed in the rightful role of the Communist Party to implement its doctrine in China.

Deng's Moderate Rule

Deng was one of the most brilliant of the original leaders of Chinese Communist Party. Having had years to think about it while working in the tractor factory, Deng defined his cardinal principles in 1959. Essentially a conservative, he said China should continue down the socialist road following the dictatorship of the proletariat and led by the Communist Party. He reemphasized the authority of Marxism-Leninism and Mao Thought. Deng said the Party "cannot be separate from the people and the people cannot be separated from the Party." With the faith of a true believer, Deng thought only the Communist Party could lead China into the future.

A revised constitution in 1978 eliminated the Four Great Freedoms, which had been (perhaps cynically) formulated by Mao. These included the right to speak freely, to fully express ones views, to debate issues, and to create wall posters.

With Deng's hand firmly on the throttle in pursuit of his Four Modernizations, there were some who believed freedom was being left in the dust. One was an electrician by the name of Wei Jingsheng, a former Red Guard. Wei pasted a large poster on the Democracy Wall near Tiananmen Square in December 1978 to protest the removal of the Four Freedoms from the Constitution.

In addition to Zhou Enlai and Deng's Four Modernizations, Wei called for a Fifth Modernization, which he defined as true democracy. Wei proclaimed democracy to be a natural, innate human right and said that anyone who took or withheld democracy was a thief. He believed the fifth modernization was essential because, without it, the others would fail.

The following month, in January 1979, the United States and China established formal diplomatic relations, and Deng visited the United States, where he was accepted as a welcome alternative to Mao. On his return, Deng found Democracy Walls spreading all across China. Thousands of young people converged on Beijing to demand human rights and democracy.

In Deng's view, democracy could only be exercised within the Communist Party, so he prohibited "slogans, posters, books, magazines, photographs, and any other material that challenged socialism, the proletarian dictatorship, the leaders of the Communist Party, Marxism-Leninism, or the thoughts of Mao Zedong." Democracy walls were prohibited.

Wei Jingsheng responded to the crackdown with an essay entitled, "Do We Want Democracy or a New Autocracy?" He warned that Deng was becoming a dictator—like Mao. Wei was arrested in the middle of the night and held for six weeks on death row. Tried without benefit of counsel, he defended himself by accusing the Party conservatives of being the "true counter-revolutionaries." They were the ones opposing the revolution for democracy.

Wei was convicted and sentenced to 15 years in prison. While his trial was secret, its verdict was broadcast across the country. He was held in solitary confinement for two years and regularly beaten. Because he refused to confess, he had to serve almost all of his sentence. We will hear more about him later.

Elections for local Party congresses were revived in 1980, and the indirectly elected National People's Congresses were allowed to have a increased influence on policy matters. Some of the most elderly members of the Politburo were forced to retire.

In 1981, the Communist Party resolved that Mao Thought constituted the Party's collective wisdom and would continue to serve as "a guide to action for a long time to come." Mao may have made some "gross mistakes," but these were outweighed by his positive contributions.

Deng's legacy is his adroit revision of Marxism-Leninism in evolving the economy from central control to market forces. He said, "To get rich is glorious."

His first step unleashed agriculture by allowing peasants to cultivate individual plots and sell their products on the open market. Under the "production responsibility system," land owned in common could be leased, and the farmer was allowed to keep or sell the surplus produced above the contracted amount. The growth rate of grain production quickly rose from 3.5 to five percent annually.

Deng's initial emphasis on heavy industry switched to consumer goods in the early 1980s, allowing foreign investment, the importation of technology, and increased foreign trade. It was a winning combination, which doubled industrial output between 1981 and 1986.

Economic policy continued to move from central planning to market forces, and price fixing was reserved for scarce materials. China had begun to accept foreign investment in 1978 and joined the International Monetary Fund. The creation of Special Economic Zones allowed foreign firms to easily invest and locate factories in China, thereby taking advantage of low wages. The government stopped funding manufacturing and let banks assume the financing of new enterprises.

With foreign trade came the need for improvements in contract law and access to courts. New law codes were adopted and law school training expanded. The Ministry of Justice was reinstituted in 1979, and the new constitution of 1982 emphasized the role of the National People's Congress as law makers and enforcers. Courts and tribunals were established and judges were appointed. There was no bill of rights, and the judiciary—as all other elements of the People's Republic of China—continued to be completely controlled by the Communist Party.

Freedom of the press, as it is known in the West, was not allowed in China. The press was, however, given a greater role in helping government root out corruption and nepotism and to provide the leadership with information about the thoughts and concerns of the masses.

Voting for local, provincial, and National People's Congress representatives was encouraged and expanded by allowing voters to have more than one choice for elective positions. Naturally, all candidates had to be vetted and approved by the Party.

Birth control, denounced as anti-Marxist during the Cultural Revolution, was revived with the imposition of a "one-child per family" policy. While nominally voluntary and encouraged by a reward of benefits, there were also sanctions for excessive children. It has been estimated that as many as 10,000,000 women were forced to have abortions each year, and hundreds of millions of men and women were sterilized under the family planning program. The birth rate declined, but China's population still passed the one billion mark in 1982.

Deng announced a policy in 1981 that Taiwan would not be recovered by force. Taiwan relaxed its foreign-exchange controls and allowed travel to the mainland, resulting in an ever-increasing rate of trade between the People's Republic of China and the Republic of China.

In 1984, Deng negotiated an agreement for the return of Hong Kong upon the expiration of England's 99-year lease in 1997. Deng promised that Hong Kong would become a Special Administrative Region and would retain its own social and economic system for another 50 years. A similar agreement was reached when Macau reverted from Portugal to China in 1999.

Under the policy of "one country, two systems," the People's Republic became responsible for defense and foreign affairs, while Hong Kong and Macau maintained their own separate legal and monetary systems. The question of free elections in Hong Kong was not fully resolved and would become an issue in the future.

Deng believed China's market economy, controlled by the Communist Party, was more stable than Western economies, because it was not subject to the election cycle. Within this span of control, the provinces and local municipalities were encouraged to invest in the enterprises they believed would be the most profitable. Investment funds came from banking and not the central government. The goal was to develop China into a fully industrialized nation.

In theory, the dictatorship of the Party will continue to guide the Chinese people along the Marxism-Leninism path—through the entanglement of capitalism and socialism—to the promised utopian pure communism in some far distant future.

The Democracy Movement and Tiananmen Square

If we recall, Wang Shiwei was the young journalist who had the audacity to criticize Mao Zedong during the Yan'an period and was hacked to death for his views. His original essay was titled "Wild Lilies," and it chastised Mao for his affairs with beautiful women and the extraordinary privileges

Deng's Moderate Rule

he and the other Party leaders enjoyed. Although Mao murdered Wang, "wild lilies" took on a life of its own, becoming the underground label of democratic dissent in China.

Conservative Party leaders became concerned in 1983 about "bourgeois liberalization" and launched a campaign against "spiritual pollution" from the West. The campaign focused on the thinking and lifestyles of students, intellectuals, artists, and writers. Hu Yaobang, then serving as the Party General Secretary, didn't agree with the campaign and looked favorably on Western influence.

The conservative campaign was doomed to failure. One reason was the resurgence of education following the Cultural Revolution. Entrance exams were once again used for admission to post-secondary institutions, and the widespread availability of radios and televisions allowed educational extension courses to reach the masses. By 1980, 1,400,000 students were enrolled in colleges and universities and millions more were receiving literacy and technical training.

Moreover, thousands of Chinese students had studied abroad and returned having experienced true free speech. Chinese scholars were talking with contemporaries in other countries. Once the door to the West was opened for trade, allowing the communication, travel, and social and cultural interaction associated with it, there was no closing it. The world was connected by satellites, and the events of the day, all over the world, were being shown on the evening television news.

In December 1986, a provincial student protest against fixed elections to the National People's Congress spread across China to Shanghai and Beijing. Party conservatives accused the progressive leader, Hu Yaobang of failing to control student demonstrations. He was forced to make self-criticisms and was removed as General Secretary. Hu remained on the Politburo, however, where he continued to urge liberal restraint.

When Hu died in April 1989, more than 10,000 Beijing students demonstrated in Tiananmen Square to honor his memory. They also protested against government corruption and called for greater transparency in the Party. Their message resonated around China.

The students organized the Beijing University Association to coordinate their protest. Among their demands was the release of Wei Jingsheng, who remained in prison. Their repeated requests to talk with the government were ignored, so they announced a boycott of classes and a general strike.

Party conservatives convinced Deng he had to take action against the protests. An editorial in the *People's Daily* referred to the student actions as turmoil and accused them of a conspiracy—words associated with the Cultural Revolution. For Deng, the demonstrations threatened his reforms, including democratization.

The editorial failed to quell the demonstrations, and large unauthorized parades took place in a number of cities on the seventieth anniversary of the May Fourth Democracy Movement. First thousands—then millions of students traveled to Tiananmen Square in Beijing to participate in the protests. They demanded greater participation of the people in their government.

Then, with the whole world watching, several thousand students began a hunger strike in Tiananmen Square—just as USSR President Mikhail Gorbachev arrived for a state visit.

The demonstrators ignored emergency orders prohibiting further demonstrations, and art students constructed a massive papier-mâché statute of the Goddess of Democracy—which they installed directly in front of Mao's portrait in the Square.

Deng feared multi-party elections would result in the kind of civil war China suffered during the Cultural Revolution. Perhaps remembering his own experience, Deng worried that Party leaders might be arrested and prosecuted. Martial law was declared and the army was called into Beijing.

The government estimated the Square was occupied by 1,200,000 students. On May 20, twenty-two divisions of the People's Liberation Army were ordered to disperse them. The people of Beijing rallied to the streets and blocked the army's path to the Square. A number of command officers refused to obey orders to move against the people.

On the night of June 3-4, six weeks after the protest started, outside provincial army units—believed to have less sympathy with the

Deng's Moderate Rule

protesters—were brought in to clear the square. The approach was once again slowed by thousands of ordinary people, who did not believe their army would ever fire on them. The soldiers did shoot into the crowd, and people began to die.

Of the millions of students who had occupied the square, only a few thousand remained. They said they were not afraid to die and had taken an oath to protect the cause of Chinese democracy. Many people had already been killed as the troops entered the square, and the army began to fire on the determined students who remained. Army tanks crushed the Goddess of Democracy under their treads.

Most of the students in the square managed to escape under a safe conduct negotiated at the last minute by Liu Xiaobo, a literary critic. Liu was arrested for his efforts, and we will hear more about him later.

At least 400 to 800 people were killed, and an unknown number were wounded. Those attempting to block the army killed 23 soldiers, wounded 7,000, and destroyed 65 trucks and 47 armored personnel carriers. The army charged more than 100 officers and 1,400 enlisted men with dereliction of duty.

The Party, threatened by the student demands for greater political participation, responded with a two-fold plan. The regime ignored the demands and the opinions of the intellectual elite. It went directly to the people with an intensive propaganda campaign that charged the demonstrators were subversives engaged in a conspiracy against the Party. Leaders were arrested and prosecuted, and those who had participated were persecuted.

There was an immediate international outcry. The United States imposed economic sanctions, curtailed weapons sales, and suspended high-level contacts; however, no nation broke diplomatic relations. International corporations paid little or no attention, as they continued to make products and money in China. Foreign investment continued to rise, and China was admitted to the World Trade Organization.

Shortly after the United States agreed to sell three communication satellites to China in January 1990, martial law was lifted, and the last 573 prisoners from Tiananmen Square were released.

The massacre at Tiananmen Square still cannot be mentioned or discussed in China's news media, and many Chinese born in the last 35 years have no knowledge of its occurrence.

Deng's Legacy

Following the events at Tiananmen Square, Deng shuffled the Party leadership, and dismissed the moderates who had supported the students. As his designated successor, he appointed the conservative hardliner Jiang Zemin to be the General Secretary. Deng later resigned his chair of the Military Commission in favor of Jiang and retired from formal leadership.

The conservative tilt of the leadership increased. The Party tried to deal with the inflation and panic following the lifting of price controls in 1988 by imposing an austerity program. Deng began to fear his liberalization of the economy was being undermined by conservative attempts to impose political and social stability. He wanted to speed up the economy, but did not have the support to do so.

Jiang was associated with the conservative elements of the leadership, and Deng was unsure what would happen when he was no longer around to protect and promote his economic plans. He argued that economic problems would become political problems—if they were not properly dealt with. In 1991, as the Communist Party began to plan for its 14th Party Conference the next year, Deng told Jiang he would support him at the Conference if increased growth was proposed. If, however, Jiang failed to act, Deng threatened to support others.

In 1992, Deng, aged 87, decided to take a grand tour of Southern China to see the new free economic zones for himself. Arriving in Wuhan, he lectured local officials on the need to solve problems, saying "whoever is against reform must leave office." In Hunan, he encouraged officials to "be bolder in carrying out reforms."

Traveling to Shenzhen and Zhuhai, Deng engaged in an 11-day inspection tour. Everywhere he went, large crowds of supporters gathered hailing him as Uncle Deng. He privately complained to local officials about the conservatives in Beijing and encouraged them to speed things up, to be bolder, to open up more. The Hong Kong media covered his visit to Shenzhen. Deng met with military planners and passed along the same message.

Jiang "got the message," thanks in part to a tape recording of the last meeting. Although conservative attempts were made to suppress articles about Deng's tour, others leaders heard what he had to say about speeding up the economy, and the alternatives. By the time Deng arrived back home, Jiang was already acknowledging the value of Deng's plan.

At the Party Congress in 1992, the building of a "socialist market economy" became the Party's plan for the next five years. Jiang elevated Deng's program to the status of "Deng Xiaoping Theory," comparable to Mao Thought.

As the Congress concluded, Deng stood next to Jiang while the media recorded the event. He took other steps to ensure Jiang's authority was not challenged and encouraged the retirement of most senior officials of Deng's generation.

In March 1993, the Politburo endorsed Deng's position. It received Jiang's full support, and he became a reliable advocate of the economic policy.

In May, the Party announced that all 30 provincial and prefectural capital cities would have the same privileges as the special zones, and 14 more cities were opened up to trade.

In one of his last exercises of power, Deng arranged for the appointment of the youngest ever member of the Politburo. His name was Hu Jintao, and he would succeed Jiang. The legacy of Deng would survive, and the Communist dynasty would continue.

Deng died in February 1997, and the tears cried by the Chinese people were real. Unlike Chairman Mao, who was deeply feared, Uncle Deng was genuinely respected. At Deng's funeral, Jiang vowed to follow his economic theory.

The country Deng Xiaoping left to posterity in 1997 was entirely different from the one he inherited from Mao Zedong twenty years earlier. Each had made their mark, for better and for worse.

The Tiger's Pragmatic Rule

The Chinese proverb "two tigers cannot share one mountain" reflects the difficulty of allocating power between strong personalities. Deng Xiaoping may have violated this principle with the manner in which he voluntarily retired. In several steps, he relinquished the power of chairing the Central Committee of the Chinese Communist Party and its Central Military Commission, to Jiang Zemin. It was not until Jiang was finally elected President in 1993, that he became the Paramount Leader of China. Even then, Deng retained great influence within the Party and government.

The situation is different in the United States, where its president automatically becomes the Commander-in-Chief of the military forces, as well as the head of state. But the U.S. president is only nominally the head of a political party. American parties do not have actual members—there are only registered voters who have expressed a political preference.

The United States was formed by joining independent states to function under a federal government, and its powers are limited by the constitution of the people (and states) that created it. China has been ruled by strong central governments for thousands of years. Today, all power in China flows down from the top of the Communist Party and is exercised in local provinces and municipalities by the corresponding Party organizations.

The Chinese Communist Party dictates the constitution and government of the People's Republic of China, and decides who its elected officials will be. With more than 86 million members, the Chinese Communist Party is the largest political party in the world, but it does not represent, nor is it elected by, the remaining 94 percent of China's 1.3 billion people. The Party dictates the agenda of the People's Congresses, and the Party decides which of its own members will be the candidates in virtually every election.

The People's Republic of China is neither a republic, nor does it belong to the people of China. It was created by and is a wholly owned subsidiary of the Chinese Communist Party—which has no intention of relinquishing, voluntarily or otherwise, its ownership or power. Any person seeking a leadership position in the party or government could not think otherwise.

Jiang Zemin (1989-2002)

Politically and economically a conservative, Jiang reluctantly supported Deng's economic policies, while promoting his own cult of personality. Jiang's ambition was to create a personal legacy, rather than be a placeholder. In his earlier office as the Mayor of Shanghai, he was considered to be a "flower pot," a person who appears useful, but who actually gets nothing done.

Keeping in mind that Deng never held the position of President, or even Premier, and sought to exercise his power outside of the limelight, Jiang attempted to control and use the Party's propaganda machinery to promote his "core of leadership" and personal contributions. The government-controlled *People's Daily* newspaper, and television programming, headlined Jiang's activities every day. He seized every opportunity to appear presidential in the Western media.

Jiang also used government media to emphasize a return to Confucian values of self-sacrifice for the public good and to encourage nationalism and patriotism in respecting the authority of the Party and the government. Even though communism was becoming increasingly difficult to justify, Jiang continued a hard line against any threat to the Party.

You may recall the imprisonment of the young electrician, Wei Jingsheng, who was convicted during the Deng regime for his poster urging true democracy as a "Fifth Modernization." He received a 15-year prison sentence and was not released until 1993, during Jiang's regime. This was shortly before his sentence was completed and only days before the decision was to be made about whether Beijing would be selected to host the 2000 Summer Olympics.

Although Wei was forbidden to talk to the press as a condition of his release, he immediately announced he would continue his fight for democracy. He wrote an article for *The New York Times* urging the United States to pressure China to respect the rights of its citizens, and he met with a U.S. human rights official.

Wei was rearrested, accused of "illegal activities under the cloak of legality," and held in secret detention. He was once again convicted and sentenced to 14 more years in prison. After serving two years, Wei was deported to the United States in 1997 for medical treatment, where he continues to live.

Jiang and the Communist Party—in which atheism is a requirement of membership—became alarmed by the rapidly growing Buddhist-inspired group known as the Falun Gong. The spiritual and moral discipline combines meditation and physical exercises with an emphasis on truthfulness, compassion, and forbearance.

Initially, the movement was supported by the Chinese government and, as its membership surpassed 100 million adherents in 1999, it requested legal recognition. Matters came to a head when 10,000 practitioners, organized through their cell phones, suddenly appeared in central Beijing to peacefully demonstrate against state interference with their religion.

Jiang decided the Falun Gong was a threat to social stability. The group was labeled a "heretical organization," and access to its Internet website was blocked. Hundreds of thousands of its followers were imprisoned, put through abusive thought reform, and required to perform forced labor. At least 3,500 died as a result of custodial abuse, and their organs were harvested for medical transplants.

Cruel and barbaric as the suppression efforts were, millions continue to secretly practice Falun Gong. Its adherents outside of China openly advocate for an end to the Communist Party dictatorship.

Trained as an engineer, rather than an economist, Jiang largely left economic policy to Wen Jiabao, the Secretary of the Central Financial Work Commission. Since China remains in the primary stage of socialism, the economic system that evolved under Jiang's rule forced a redefinition of traditional Marxism. Now defined as socialism with Chinese characteristics, the Chinese socialist market economy remains under state control and the dictatorship of the Communist Party. The current primary state of socialism is expected to last for another 100 years.

Jiang's contribution to posterity was his formulation of a political and economic theory, formally known as the Three Represents, which was incorporated into China's constitution:

> This experience and the historical experiences gained by the Party since its founding can be summarized as follows: Our Party must always represent the requirements for developing China's advanced productive forces, the orientation of China's advanced culture, and the fundamental interests of the overwhelming majority of the Chinese people. These are the inexorable requirements for maintaining and developing socialism, and the logical conclusion our Party has reached through hard exploration and great praxis.

The avowed purpose of Jiang's theory was to make the Communist Party more democratic by opening up its membership to "the overwhelming majority of the Chinese people." This means, in the context of the present political reality, the advanced productive forces, (the business class, or capitalists), the advanced culture (an educated, upwardly mobile elite), and the rest of the people.

Jiang's doctrine did not leave many, if any, classes left to struggle against. In fact, "class struggle" has been replaced by "economic development" as the central focus of the Party's doctrine.

By 2004, 30 percent of the new entrepreneurs had joined the Party, and almost one quarter of the membership is now composed of "managing, professional, and technical staff in enterprises and public institutions."

The Tiger's Pragmatic Rule

The formal criteria for membership has evolved from a strictly ideological requirement of "redness" to one that emphasizes educational and technical expertise. Nonetheless, probationary members must still take the oath of allegiance:

> It is my will to join the Communist Party of China, uphold the Party's program, observe the provisions of the Party constitution, fulfill a Party member's duties, carry out the Party's decisions, strictly observe Party discipline, guard Party secrets, be loyal to the Party, work hard, fight for communism throughout my life, be ready at all times to sacrifice my all for the Party and the people, and never betray the Party.

The Party encouraged people to work hard and get rich, but exactly how they were to go about this was not clearly defined. Far too many bureaucrats, officials and Party members—as well as their friends and families—found many ways to get rich, without having to work too hard. The problems started at the top and worked themselves all the way to the bottom. The Communist Party, which once prided itself on being so much cleaner than the venal Nationalist regime, found itself riddled with corruption.

Once Jiang became Paramount Leader of China, he promoted a number of his former cronies from Shanghai to positions of power within the Party. These appointments provided him with political support, but it also gave them the chance to sell their influence to the highest bidder and direct government funds and contracts to their own friends and families. While these activities were not apparent to the public, other Party members were quick to grasp what was happening around them and lost no time getting in line to get rich quick. As much as ten percent of China's Gross National Product was diverted, annually, by corrupt officials in the government and military.

The extent of corruption had yet to be revealed in 1998, when Jiang's leadership was confirmed for another five years at a Party congress, and Hu Jintao was elevated to Vice President.

In keeping with the multi-staged succession process initiated by Deng Xiaoping, Jiang handed over the chair of the Politburo Standing Committee and appointed Hu Jintao as General Secretary in 2002. Jiang resigned as chairman of the Party Central Military Commission two years later.

Hu Jintao (2002-2012)

Hu Jintao's mother was a teacher, and his father, who owned a successful tea trading business, was persecuted during the Cultural Revolution. Hu graduated with a degree in water conservancy engineering in 1965 and was employed as an engineer by Sinohydro, the state-owned engineering and construction company. He was active in Communist Party activities and managed Party affairs in the Ministry of Water Resources and Electric Power.

Deng Xiaoping instituted a program in 1980 calling for the development of younger, more revolutionary, more knowledgeable and more specialized Party leaders. Hu and Wen Jiabao, who would became Hu's Premier in 2003, were identified for Deng's personnel development program by a nation-wide talent search.

Hu moved quickly through Party positions, particularly in the Communist Youth League, where he was ultimately appointed leader of the Youth League Central Committee. Equipped with a photographic memory, Hu continued to be assigned to increasingly more responsible positions, until he was appointed to the highest Party post in the Tibetan Autonomous Region in 1988. He arrived just in time to be confronted with riots on the 30th anniversary of the Tibetan revolt. Martial law was declared, and the police brutally suppressed the riot with gunfire. Several Tibetans were killed.

Hu's actions were a prelude to the Tiananmen Square massacre, which occurred three months later. He supported the Party's hard line response and gained Deng's recognition. When Hu returned to Beijing, he was selected by Deng for the seven-member Politburo Standing Committee

The Tiger's Pragmatic Rule

in 1992, the youngest to have ever served on the Committee. Hu became head of the Secretariat and was put in charge of the Party's ideological work at the Central Party School.

Having been groomed as a Party leader, Hu was initially appointed as the Vice President of China in 1998 and began to take a leading role in foreign affairs. In keeping with Deng's succession plan, Hu became the General Secretary in 2002.

Even though Hu became Paramount Leader in 2004, his effective power was diluted by the remaining majority of Jiang's Shanghai appointees on the Politburo Standing Committee. Like Deng, Jiang attempted to influence events from behind the curtain.

Just because Hu was a pragmatist on economic matters, did not mean he was necessarily a liberal on political and social issues. To better understand Hu's policy on dissent, let us recall another youth leader who was imprisoned for his political beliefs and activities following Tiananmen Square. Liu Xiaobo, a writer, literary critic, and professor, negotiated the last minute escape of many of the students.

Although Liu had urged the students to engage in dialogue, rather than class struggle, and managed to save many lives, he was imprisoned for more than a year and convicted of "counter-revolutionary propaganda and incitement." Liu's sentence was commuted because he had helped avoid a greater loss of life at Tiananmen Square.

Not allowed to publish in China, Liu Xiaobo continued to write and publish overseas. He was arrested in May 1995 for petitioning the government to reconsider the Tiananmen Square protests and take appropriate steps toward political reform. He was released after nine months of home detention.

Within months of his release, Liu was rearrested for advocating a peaceful reunification with Taiwan, rather than a military invasion. His statements were deemed to disturb the public order, and he was confined for two years of re-education through labor.

Following Liu's release in 1999, he published a book in Hong Kong titled *A Nation That Lies to Conscience*. His telephone and Internet lines were monitored. When he started writing a human rights report about China in 2004, his computer and writing materials were seized. He was placed under house arrest in January 2005 for supporting student demonstrations.

His last and final confrontation with the Party occurred in 2008, when Liu helped write and circulate a political declaration calling for a greater freedom of expression, human rights, true democratic elections, privatization of state lands and industries, and a more liberal economic system. It did not call for the abolishment of the Communist Party, only that other political parties be allowed to oppose it during free elections.

Liu and 300 other political activists signed Charter 08, which was to be launched on the 60th anniversary of the Universal Declaration of Human Rights.

The day before the scheduled release, Liu was arrested by the police and all of his computers were seized. Nonetheless, the declaration was circulated on the Internet by others and was signed by thousands before the authorities managed to block it.

Kept in solitary confinement and denied access to counsel, Liu was charged with suspicion of inciting subversion of state power and subverting the socialist system. The state media reported he had confessed to spreading false rumors and slander.

Following a trial at which Liu was not allowed to speak, he was convicted and sentenced to eleven years of imprisonment. There was an outpouring of international condemnation of the sentence, including formal appeals for his release by the United States and the European Union. Liu was nominated for the Nobel Peace Prize by the 14th Dalai Lama, Desmond Tutu, and other notables. He was awarded the Prize in October 2010 "for his long and non-violent struggle for fundamental human rights in China."

The news of the award was censored in China, where the government considered Liu to be an undeserving criminal. Liu's wife was held under house arrest, and many of his friends and associates were placed under surveillance. Liu remains in Jinzhou Prison.

The Tiger's Pragmatic Rule

The discussion of democracy in China seems schizophrenic. Hu mentioned democracy more than 61 times during a speech in 2007, and he described democracy as a common objective of humanity. Nonetheless, the timetable for implementing real democracy remains entirely at the discretion of the Communist Party and is not subject to question. Any complaint about the style of democracy provided by the Party is tantamount to treason.

In its attempt to justify how six percent of the population can dictate the lives of the other 94 percent, the Party strains to explain: "Without the Communist Party, there would be no new China. Nor would there be people's democracy." This doctrine is known as Democratic centralism. As a modern version of Mao's Mass Line, it holds that the Party listens to the people and considers their needs in making correct decisions on behalf of the public interest. The Party is "against the anarchic call for democracy for all."

Hu Jintao continued Jiang's pivot from communism to nationalism and patriotism in calling for a Socialist Harmonious Society. He defined such a society as one in which every person strives for harmony, even to the detriment of his or her own rights and best interests. Social harmony in the new capitalistic economy begins to sound a lot like fascism.

Hu also expressed the idea of the Shadow of the Future, saying "The young are the future of a nation and the hopes of the world." The youth of China may or may not feel they have the power to do (or say) anything about the future of their nation due to the widespread suppression of any hint of dissent on the Internet and modern social media. When a censored comment or other objectionable posting in China suddenly disappears from cyberspace, it is said to have been "harmonized." The Internet in China is closely monitored by an many as 250,000 censors.

By personality, Hu is a quiet and self-contained person. He maintained a very low personal profile during his tenure in office while allowing China to be opened up to the world. He learned from the condemnation of the Party's suppression and denial of the deadly SARS (severe acute respiratory syndrome) epidemic the year he took office in 2002.

Afterwards, Hu personally directed the open media coverage and acceptance of outside assistance following the massive Sichuan earthquake in May 2008—that killed almost 70,000 people. Uncomfortable as he may have personally felt, a few months later he proudly welcomed the world to the 2008 Beijing Summer Olympics.

Hu's philosophy was: "Don't rock the boat; don't make any changes." But, the turbulent waters of Party corruption were doing more than rocking Hu's boat as he neared the end of his leadership voyage.

In February 2012, just before turning over the General Secretary chair of the Central Committee to his Vice President, Hu received a telephone call about an armed standoff between different police forces outside the U.S. Consulate in Chongqing, one of China's five major cities. The Chief of Police was seeking political asylum, and the Mayor was trying to kidnap him to keep him quiet about a murder committed by the Mayor's wife. It had all the drama of a soap opera and was a good introduction to what was to confront the next Paramount Leader.

Xi Jinping (2012-Present)

Xi is one of China's "Princelings," as the children of senior Party leaders are known by the Chinese people. Others have amassed great fortunes through corruption, but Xi was the first Princeling to become Paramount Leader of China. His father, Xi Zhongxun, had already established a communist base in northwest China when Mao arrived there after the Long March. Xi Zhongxun went on to hold a number of senior Party positions, including vice-premier under Zhou Enlai. Like other senior leaders, he was persecuted during the Cultural Revolution and later rehabilitated by Deng Xiaoping.

Xi Jinping's secondary education was interrupted when his school was closed by the Cultural Revolution. Sent into the countryside to work, he became the Party secretary of the local production team. He was able to continue his education in 1975 and studied practical chemical engineering, before moving on to Marxist philosophy and law. He is said to have obtained a Doctorate of Law in 2002, but there is strong evidence the degree was fabricated from the published works of others to polish up Xi's poor educational record.

Xi's political career was a succession of increasingly important Party positions in the provinces, before becoming party chief and governor of Zhejiang province. There, he made a name for himself by his prosecution of corruption. In 2007, Xi was moved to Shanghai to be its Party Secretary, which accorded him a seat on the Standing Committee of the Politburo.

In October 2010, Xi was appointed Vice-Chairman of the Central Military Commission, the first step toward leading the Party. This was followed two years later by his becoming General Secretary and Chairman of its Central Military Committee.

Xi has defined the "Chinese Dream" as an expectation of the people for "better education, more stable jobs, better income, more reliable social security, medical care of a higher standard, more comfortable living conditions, and a more beautiful environment." With a nod towards nationalism, Xi says, "to realize the renaissance of the Chinese Nation is the greatest dream for the Chinese Nation in modern history."

Since becoming President of China and Paramount Leader in March 2013, Xi has dared young people "to dream, work assiduously to fulfill the dreams and contribute to the revitalization of the nation." He wants young people to "cherish the glorious youth, strive with pioneer spirit and contribute their wisdom and energy to the realization of the Chinese dream."

The dream does not, however, include any relaxation of the sacrosanct domination of all politics by the Communist Party. Xi repeatedly reminds listeners that reforms can occur only with the Party's strong authoritarian leadership. His administration reserves the right to send television and film personnel on involuntary visits to rural areas to help them "form a correct view of art and create more masterpieces."

An official document of the Party warns about dangerous Western values, including constitutional democracy and universal human rights, and it prohibits their discussion in educational materials. Universities are directed to "enhance guidance over thinking and keep a tight grip on leading ideological work in higher education." They are urged to "enhance their sense of dangers and resolutely safeguard political security and ideological security."

Xi has written, "Never allow singing to a tune contrary to the party center," and "Never allow eating the Communist Party's food and then smashing the Communist Party's cooking pots." Professors and journalists who support multi-party elections or question the wisdom of Mao find themselves marginalized or without employment.

The official Communist Party media accuses the West of conspiring to overthrow the Party and attempts to lay the blame for domestic disturbances on the "black hand" of "hostile foreign forces."

Xi has been more concerned about the corruption of Party officials than democracy for the masses. Focusing on the need to combat corruption and control China's massive internal security mechanism, Xi organized and chairs a new National Security Commission and the Central Leading Group for Comprehensively Deepening Reforms. He has been phasing out the notorious gulag system of re-education through labor.

In January 2013, Xi vowed he would spear tigers and swat flies in targeting both top officials and lowly bureaucrats in his anti-corruption drive. He said, "We must uphold the fighting of tigers and flies at the same time, resolutely investigating law-breaking cases of leading officials and also earnestly resolving the unhealthy tendencies and corruption problems which happen all around people." He promised there would be no exceptions, or leniency, in the campaign.

Targets for the "comprehensively deepening reforms" popped up all over the place as Xi took office. The first major scandal had occupied Hu in the closing days of his administration, and was left for Xi to clean up.

Bo Xilai, another Princeling, had been promoted to Party Secretary and Mayor of Chongquing (Chungking), which had served as the capital of China during the Japanese occupation. With a population in excess of 33 million, it is one of the five major core cities under the direct control of Beijing.

The Tiger's Pragmatic Rule

Bo, a conservative neo-Maoist member of the Politburo, was on the fast track for a place on its Standing Committee and greater national responsibilities. His mentor was Zhou Yongkang, Jiang's head of the State Security Ministry and chairman of the Politics and Law Commission. Zhou was the third most powerful person in China. With an allocation that exceeded the defense budget, Zhou directly commanded more than ten million national, provincial, and local law enforcement officers, including the armed anti-riot paramilitary force. Bo was Zhou's designated successor.

Using his chief of police as an attack dog, Bo engaged in a vicious anti-crime and corruption battle, resulting in the torture and execution of hundreds of suspects. At the same time, his wife used his influence and her law practice to represent billionaires in land and business transactions. She raked in millions from the deals, which she moved offshore.

A falling out with an English consultant—who helped Bo's wife launder funds—resulted in a plot by the wife and chief of police to kill the Englishman. Things began to unravel after the murder, when the chief of police tried to blackmail Bo and his wife to secure a promotion. Bo refused and the chief, fearing for his life, sought political asylum at the U.S. Consulate.

The story was picked up and reported by offshore Chinese-language publications and began to flash around Weibo, China's primary social media network. Bo was removed as Party leader in Chongquing, and he and his wife were placed under investigation by the Central Commission for Discipline Inspection (which concerns itself with top officials).

Bo's wife confessed, and she and the chief were convicted at a trial with no witnesses and little due process. She received a suspended death sentence, and the chief got 15 years of imprisonment. Bo remained under investigation, and his mentor, Zhou Yongkang, the Party's internal security czar, was targeted.

Stories began to circulate about Zhou's support of Bo, his womanizing, and his possible role in the "accidental" death of his first wife—which allowed Zhou to marry an attractive young television personality. Zhou used his power to block reporting of the stories on the Internet, and State Security hackers began to attack offshore Chinese-language news outlets which carried them.

The accounts continued to spread and become more focused. It seems there was a plot for Bo to succeed Zhou Yongkang, secure a seat on the Standing Committee of the Politburo and take down Xi Jinping, who was scheduled to become Paramount Leader. Zhou was involuntarily retired under the unwritten rule that members of the Politburo Standing Committee are not subject to investigation.

Bo's case was finally brought to trial in September 2013, and he was convicted of bribery, abuse of power, and corruption. Bo was sentenced to life imprisonment and expelled from the Party.

Setting aside the rule against investigating members of the Politburo Standing Committee, Xi formed a special task force to scrutinize the activities of Zhou Yongkang, who was placed under house arrest. He was finally taken into custody in August 2014 for "grave violations of discipline." The more serious crimes of corruption, murder, and plotting a coup against Xi may never be publically revealed.

Earlier in April 2012, in response to the Bo scandal, *The New York Times* reported on comments by Chinese Premier Wen Jiabao, the most senior official pushing the Bo investigation and prosecution. In an article titled, "Let Power be Exercised in the Sunshine," Wen said "the biggest danger to a political party in power is corruption." He went on to say, "the dignity and authority of the law cannot be trampled," and "There is no special citizen before the law."

Just six months later, in October 2012, the *Times* reported the results of an extensive journalistic investigation of Wen Jiabao and his family—which Chinese diplomats had attempted to spike before publication. (Within two hours, access to the article on the Internet was blocked in China.) The story details how Wen's family came to control $2.7 billion in assets during the time Wen was in power. Even his 90-year-old mother had a book value of $120 million.

Wen's response, through his lawyers, was that the article was inaccurate and based on leaks from Bo supporters. The article was, however,

The Tiger's Pragmatic Rule

entirely based on independent research by the *Times*. Moreover, while Wen had supported a requirement that senior leaders reveal the full extent of their family's financial holdings to the Party, he has yet to personally make such information publicly available. This suggests the *Times* article was close to the mark. Wen has since retired.

Inasmuch as there were rumors that Zhou Yongkang actually attempted to assassinate Xi on two occasions, it is understandable that Xi has been purging those members of the Jiang faction who pose the greatest physical threat. Moreover, since it is unlikely Bo, Zhou, and others would have plotted against Xi without Jiang's encouragement or acquiescence, it appears Xi is zeroing in on Jiang personally. Xi's taskforce has set up an office in Shanghai, Jiang's hometown. One of its first arrests was a close friend of Jiang, a wealthy businessman, for embezzlement and bribery.

The Central Commission for Discipline Inspection has announced that 6,000 senior Communist Party officials have been taken down in the anti-corruption campaign, and thousands more are under investigation. The Commission punished 84,000 Party members for discipline infractions in just the first half of 2014. With the arrest of the very highest officials and their "forceful" interrogation (without a presumption of innocence or right to remain silent), a direct connection to Jiang will undoubtedly be established. Whether or not he is ever prosecuted, or only suffers a loss of face, remains to be seen.

An unspoken issue in these investigations was Jiang's violent persecution of the Fulun Gong, which involved the participation of many of the suspects. Thousands of Fulun Gong members were killed and their body organs were harvested for medical transplants. One estimate is that more than 62,000 may have been murdered for organs. Irrespective of other problems that may confront him, Xi does not appear to have been involved in what may be one of history's most gruesome crimes against humanity. Whether he chooses to reveal the full extent of the macabre conspiracy remains to be seen.

A June 2012 article in *Bloomberg News* (that was quickly blocked on the Internet in China) reported Xi's extended family (excluding him, his wife and his daughter) had large investments in companies, with more than a billion dollars in assets. Primarily held by his older sister, her husband, and their daughter, the family's net worth could not be fully determined. The article quotes Xi as warning officials to "Rein in your spouses, children, relatives, friends, and staff, and vow not to use power for personal gain." Subsequent reporting by *The New York Times* in 2014 indicates Xi family members are actively divesting themselves of assets to reduce their political and criminal vulnerability.

Xi, like Bo, is a Princeling from a revolutionary family. He is generally conservative and unlikely to change. Currently engaged in a purge of opponents in an effort to secure his power base, Xi's success may depend on his balancing military support with combating corruption in the army.

Under the reign of Mao Zedong, the People's Liberation Army was encouraged to engage in state-run businesses to help pay for itself. While many of these enterprises have been phased out, China's own style of a military-industrial complex has provided ample opportunity for malfeasance. Xi sees military corruption as interfering with his goal of fielding a professional combat-ready force capable of standing up to the United States. One high-ranking officer has already been convicted of embezzlement, bribery, and abuse of power, and others are under investigation.

Just like China's civil government, the army is subject to Party control and is an extension of the Party's power. In second place behind the United States, China has been raising its military budget each year in an attempt to project its power into the areas that concern it.

Xi may have secured the powerful chairmanship of the Central Military Commission, but a large contingent of the military remains committed to the conservative Jiang faction. This includes command of troops in the Beijing and Guangzhou military regions, who may have been involved in plotting the coup against Xi. Loyalty to Jiang has to be smashed, if Xi is to have the full power of a paramount leader.

Despite his royal upbringing, Xi is attempting to create an image of being at one with the ordinary people of China. He is encouraging a cult

The Tiger's Pragmatic Rule

of personality showing off "Uncle Xi," his beautiful and talented wife, and their lovely children. The Party propaganda machine operates nonstop in churning out articles extolling Xi's virtues. A music video depicts his as a model husband and citizen; a musical about his life is playing in a Beijing theatre; art students have to draw his portrait as a part of their entrance examination; and a ditty about Uncle Xi says that he dares to beat any tiger and is not afraid of heaven or earth.

Xi presides over two nations. More than 300 million Chinese have migrated to the urban areas in the last 30 years, and 160 cities now have populations exceeding one million. In the northern area around Beijing and along the Pacific coast, some people are getting rich and others are living better. In the central and western areas, particularly in Tibet, where Buddhism is practiced, and Xinjiang, where Islam is followed, living standards have not improved, and many people live on the edge of starvation under heavy political and police repression.

In January 2014, authorities arrested Ilham Tohti, a Uyghur economics professor in Beijing on charges of separatism. Tohti is a moderate, who became well-known for advocating increased democratic rights for all Chinese people, including Muslims and Tibetans. He did not seek to separate the formerly independent northwest province of Xinjiang from China. Tohti was convicted in September 2014 and sentenced to life in prison. Seven students who worked on Tohti's website have also been charged with separatism.

The Gini coefficient is considered one of the most accurate measures of income disparity in every country. It uses a scale of zero to one, with higher decimal numbers representing the greatest disparity. For China in 1980, the measure was 0.3, and it rose to 0.5 in 2010. This midpoint of the scale reveals a severe gap between the rich and poor and is considered to be a reliable prediction of social unrest. The most recent calculation is an astounding 0.74, and, indeed, social unrest is occurring throughout China.

During this same approximate period, the number of officially reported protests (more than 100 people involved) rose from 8,500 in

1993, to 87,000 in 2005, and to 120,000 in 2008. It is conservatively estimated more than 100,000 serious protests are now taking place every year, which means hundreds of thousands of people are protesting thousands of times a year in China about matters that directly concern them. These include being kicked off of their land, locked out of their place of work without being paid, or having to breath air so thick with pollution people cannot see where they are going.

Reported incidents are primarily peasant and working-class riots, but the middle-class is also distressed. Similar to the situation in the United States, the top one percent of Chinese citizens own one-third of the nation's wealth, while the bottom one-fourth are left with only one percent of the wealth. More than 643,000 Chinese are now ranked as millionaires.

The poor, working, and middle classes subsidize the growth of wealth in China with the poor quality of the air they breathe and water they drink. In its rush towards industrialization and foreign trade, China is quickly closing on the United States, as the greatest consumer of energy. Unfortunately, much of China's energy is derived from the burning of dirty coal—making China one of the most polluted places on Earth. As early as 2007, it was reported that air pollution was causing 300,000 deaths each year, which is predicted to rise to 550,000 by 2020. Half of the population does not have access to safe drinking water, and China is generally suffering from severe water shortages.

It is not enough to crack down on corruption; the system which allowed it to flourish must also be brought into line through laws and regulations establishing the limits of permissible behavior, both commercially and personally. More and more young people are receiving legal educations, including the new Premier, Li Keqiang.

Employment and business regulations are being imposed and legal standards are being established to comply with the economic due process requirements of international trade. One example is the Labor Law of 2008, which extended layoff protection and benefits to workers. It was not, however, fairly enforced during the recession that immediately followed its enactment.

The Tiger's Pragmatic Rule

As the civil justice system becomes better established and institutionalized, more Chinese people are hiring lawyers and taking their civil disputes to court. This process is currently being tolerated by the Communist Party, as it does not directly threaten its power. Whether individuals have or should have an equal right to challenge unjust regulations and laws that deprive them of their personal freedoms of expression, assembly, and religion is an entirely different question. These rights may exist in the constitution, but they do not currently exist in practice, nor will they ever exist as long as the Communist Party retains the dictatorial power to unilaterally amend the constitution to conform to its latest doctrine.

Xi's battle against corruption is well publicized, but less well known is his repression of independent civic groups, such as those advocating for workers' rights, feminists striving for equality, scholars seeking academic freedom, or journalists who leak "state secrets" involving human rights violations. Human rights attorneys were targeted in a crackdown on dissent in July 2015, and more than 200 were detained. Members of the "rights defense" movement were charged with subversion and "wrecking the rule of law and disturbing social order." Most were ultimately released, but 12 human rights attorneys have "disappeared," and their families have no knowledge of their whereabouts.

Heavy surveillance of the Internet is increasingly resulting in detentions of individuals for "picking quarrels and provoking trouble" by criticizing the Communist Party and other online speech found to be objectionable. Five young feminists were detained for attempting to organize a campaign against sexual abuse, and others have been arrested under an "anti-rumor campaign" for questioning the official version of news events.

Chinese activists urged President Obama to cancel his invitation for Xi Jinping's visit to the United States in September 2015. The visit went off as planned, however, protesters, including members of the Falun Gong, were present at each of his stops. His appearance at a United Nations meeting on gender equality was criticized as "shameless" by former Secretary of State and presidential candidate, Hillary Clinton because of his prosecution of feminist activists in China.

Whether Xi succeeds or not as Paramount Leader depends on whether he has the foresight to recognize the legitimacy of the people's concerns about social and economic matters and their freedom to live in a truly democratic nation.

The remaining question is whether the Communist Party will come to realize that the full potential of the Chinese people cannot and will not ever be realized until the people are given the freedom to think for themselves. That issue will be addressed in the next part.

Part Three: China and the United States

Changing Course

The relationship of China with the United States has been somewhat different from that of the other imperialist and corporate powers which invaded China in the Nineteenth Century. At least it has been more nuanced. It has certainly been unique.

Like the other mercantile nations, the United States was seeking to open up markets for its corporations to make a profit. As the world's leading democracy, however, the United States was also seeking to demonstrate the power that flows from freedom.

The thousands of American missionaries who traveled to China took more than the *Bible* with them—they also preached the advantages of a government that provides the freedom of religion. They used simplified Chinese written characters to print their message; they were listened to, and English became known throughout China. Even though there was a time when Mao Zedong tried to switch the second language of China to Russian, a knowledge of English by Chinese students is now a requirement for university admission. Officially, it is the only major second language studied in China.

Although the United States was one of the allied powers during the Boxer Rebellion and was granted a share of China's indemnity, the U.S. Congress legislated that the money should be used to establish a scholarship program for Chinese students. More than one thousand came to study in America, most of whom returned home to provide valuable services to China.

An Essential History of China

The battle against Japan during World War II was primarily fought and won by American and Chinese troops. Following the war, the United States made a substantial effort to avoid a resumption of China's civil war by encouraging the formation of a unified communist and nationalist government.

The low point in relations between the United States and China came during the Korean War when Mao dispatched millions of Chinese troops to aid North Korea in its invasion of South Korea. Chinese and American families suffered the deaths of hundreds of thousands of their children in one of history's most senseless wars—as the final line drawn between North and South Korea was at the very same place it was when the war began.

China was isolated for the next 20 years, as Mao broke off relations with the Soviet Union and the rest of the world, resulting in the deaths of millions of Chinese from famine and neglect. Mao particularly held the United States in low regard, "If the U.S. monopoly capitalist groups persist in pushing their policies of aggression and war, the day is bound to come when they will be hanged by the people of the whole world."

Mao never forgave the United States, but, as a political realist, he welcomed President Richard Nixon, the old "red-baiter," to China in 1972. The United States established diplomatic relations with China in 1979, transferring its formal national recognition from the Republic of China on Taiwan to the People's Republic of China.

Since then, American corporations have invested billions of dollars in industrial production facilities on the Chinese mainland, and the United States has become China's most important trading partner. The U.S. trade deficit with China in 2013 exceeded $318.7 billion, and it amounted to $254 billion in just the first half of 2014. China is the largest foreign holder of U.S. treasury bills, notes, and bonds, currently valued at $1.2 trillion.

Other than trade disputes and conflicting monetary policies, which, to a certain extent, is business as usual, the primary irritant between the United States and China at the moment centers around the territorial status of some small islands in the East China and South China Seas.

Changing Course

Threats of War

The present dispute is between China and its neighbors, including Japan, the Philippines, Taiwan, and Vietnam. The strategic value of small reefs and islands off the shores of these nations lies in the ability of claiming countries to expand their international boundaries to include the islands and surrounding areas, some of which hold subsurface petroleum reserves. Among other things, China is relying on maps from the Ming dynasty, which identified some of the islands.

China claims an Exclusive Economic Zone that includes most of the South China Sea. Its zone hugs the shore of Vietnam, runs southward almost to Brunei and Indonesia, and extends eastward almost to the Philippines. It also includes all of Taiwan and overlaps Japan's Economic Zone in the East China Sea.

The Senkaku islands are at the tail end of a string of islands, including Okinawa, that sweep southward from Japan toward Taiwan. These islands were seized from China, along with Taiwan, by Japan following the Sino-Japanese War. They were temporarily occupied by the United States following World War II and later returned to Japan. China's air defense zone now includes these islands, and warplanes from both nations have been playing dangerous tag games in the sky over them.

As accusations fly back and forth, the United States has aligned itself with Japan and encouraged it to step up its military defenses. The Japanese government responded with a new interpretation of its pacifistic constitution (imposed by the U.S. at the end of World War II) which bans the use of armed forces, except in self-defense. The United States and Japan have integrated their cyber and ballistic missile defense systems, and the Japanese government now says it is now prepared to defend the interests of the United States, as well as its own.

Further south, China and Vietnam are disputing the ownership of some of the Paracel islands in the South China Sea, which Vietnam claims are within its Exclusive Economic Zone. China responded in May 2014 by anchoring a deep ocean drilling platform off one of the islands, guarded by a flotilla of ships.

Chinese and Vietnamese patrol vessels bumped into one another, and accusations were made. China finally withdrew its drilling equipment and suggested the parties negotiate the issues and discuss trade. The United States eased its embargo on arms sales to Vietnam and promised to provide it with additional naval patrol boats to defend itself. Vietnam has already purchased six submarines from Russia and is negotiating with U.S. and Europeans arms suppliers to buy new fighter jets, patrol planes, and drones.

To the east, China and the Philippines dispute sovereignty over some of the Spratly islands. The Philippine navy has been arresting Chinese fishermen for poaching, and the Chinese navy has been blocking resupply of a beached Philippine navy vessel on one of the island shoals. The United States signed an Enhanced Defense Cooperation Agreement with the Philippines, reaffirming it will come to the defense of the Philippines in the South China Sea.

U.S. spy satellite photographs in April 2015 revealed that China is engaged in a major dredging operation to transform five small coral reef into artificial islands in the Spratley Island group. The artificial islands, which include harbors and military aircraft runways, are being equipped with defensive artillery weapons systems. Recent low-level reconnaissance flights by U.S. spy planes over the islands have been repeatedly warned off by Chinese authorities.

By attempting to impose a military exclusion zone, China is creating "facts on the ground" supporting its claim to sovereignty in the South China Sea. The United States has responded by sending military aircraft and ships to the area—which further increases the risk of confrontation.

In October 2015, the United States deployed a guided-missile destroyer near one of the artificial islands to assert the freedom of navigation. Secretary of Defense Ash Carter warned, "We will fly, sail, and operate wherever international law permits." Speaking through a state-run newspaper, the Chinese government proclaimed it "is not frightened to fight a war with the U.S. in the region and is determined to safeguard its national interests and dignity."

China has ratified the United Nations Convention of the Law of the Sea, which establishes the freedom of navigation. Ironically, the United

Changing Course

States has declined to ratify the treaty arguing that it would interfere with America's capacity for self-government and self defense. The Philippines has filed a claim over the Spratly Island group in the Permanent Court of Arbitration in The Hague; however, China claims the Court does not have jurisdiction over the matter and refuses to participate in the proceedings. The Court has ruled against China's claim.

Inasmuch as communism has become almost impossible to defend, the last three Chinese paramount leaders have increasingly relied on patriotism and nationalism to stir up support from the masses. Disputes over islands in the China seas make for good headlines and propaganda in the Party-controlled media.

On the other side of the Pacific, President Obama has issued his own appeal to patriotism and nationalism in proclaiming America's "exceptionalism." Under his leadership, the United States has "pivoted to Asia," and the U.S. is expanding its military relationships with China's neighbors in order to "contain" Chinese ambitions. Of course, China says it cannot be contained and has been negotiating security guarantees with neighboring Russia, Iran, Pakistan and India. With its Eurasian Economic Union with Russia, Belarus, Kazakhstan, and Armenia, China is establishing modern economic Silk Roads into and through Central Asia, which will include roads, pipelines, and high-speed rail lines.

China is now deploying submarines with nuclear missile capabilities, testing rockets capable of destroying American satellites, and planning trips to the moon. President Xi called on the People's Liberation Army to "strive to establish a new military doctrine, institutions, equipment systems, strategies and tactics and management modes" for information warfare. The United States replied by indicting five Chinese army officers for hacking computer systems in the U.S. and by stepping up its own electronic warfare capability.

China's 2.3 million-strong armed forces are the world's largest and are engaged in a rapid modernization program—aided by U.S. allies. Israel has been China's major supplier of high-tech equipment in the past, but the European Union has relaxed its embargo of arms exports to China, and its air force is about to receive France's latest helicopters. Russia is in the process of selling its top-of-the-line jet fighters to China and will probably share its latest air defense anti-missile systems.

China is rapidly expanding its navy to confront the carrier-based fleets deployed by the United States in the region. While it presently has only one carrier, which it converted from a Russian ship, China appears to be considering more. It has also constructed a fleet of submarines powered by German engines and three new nuclear-powered submarines. These subs are equipped with powerful anti-ship missiles that can challenge carrier-based fleets. Moreover, China has constructed the world's largest coast guard fleet—deploying more patrol boats than the combined forces of all of its neighbors around the North and South China Seas. The United States may still be fighting World War II in deploying massive and expensive aircraft carriers—that can be quickly destroyed by powerful anti-ship missiles fired from more agile submarines and China's large fleet of fast frigates and destroyers.

Blaming the United States for "meddling in South China Sea affairs," a policy paper issued in May 2015 promulgated China's strategy to extend its naval power beyond the China Seas. The paper states, "The traditional mentality that land outweighs sea must be abandoned, and great importance has to be attached to managing the seas and oceans and protecting maritime rights and interests."

Nobody wants to go to war over some tiny little islands, but threats get made, fears get aroused, someone's pride get offended, and mistakes happen. The heat's rising in the China Seas, and it's time to turn down the thermostat.

What Can Be Done?

With the foreign policy of both the United States and China heavily influenced by neo-conservatives (who share a belief in the power of the military-security-intelligence-industrial complex to solve national problems), suggested alternatives to violence may seem remote or naive. If, however, we can determine what the people of the two nations really want and deserve, and if we honestly look at the successes and failures of both governments, we may find some common ground.

Whether or not the United States is really exceptional, one thing is certain—it should solve its own internal problems before seeking to impose its solutions on other nations.

The Failed Economic and Political Systems of the United States and China

Along with Cuba, Laos, Vietnam, and North Korea, China is one of the last remaining political experiments using Marxism to justify a single-party dictatorship. Even so, China and the others (except North Korea) have all joined the World Trade Organization and have been forced by reality to embrace capitalism in one form or another in order to survive. All other countries that tried Marxism-Leninism—including Russia, where it originated—have abandoned the experiment as a failure.

China's attempt to blend market forces with state controls has resulted in its having the worst of both systems. On one hand, in the rush to get rich, the disparity between the wealthy and the poor exceeds that found at any earlier time during the rule of the Communist Dynasty, and it is rapidly increasing. On the other hand, the repression required for its single-party dictatorship to remain in power is just another manifestation of the cruelty suffered by the Chinese people during their 4,000 years of dynastic rule.

Moreover, by using U.S. capitalism as a model, China is adopting a system that is also a failure. While President Xi is chasing the China Dream, for many in the United States, the American Dream is a distant memory.

The Gini coefficient of income disparity in United States is currently at .378, which is half that of China. Nonetheless, the U.S. coefficient has been steadily rising over the past 30 years and is currently among the highest of all developed nations. The last time things were this bad was just before the Great Depression, yet it has not always been this way.

During the era of the American Dream, from the end of the Second World War and into the mid-1970s, the bottom 90 percent of Americans were receiving almost 70 percent of the income. Today, the bottom 90 percent gets less than half. The top ten percent shares the other half, with the top one percent raking in almost a quarter of total income.

Another way of looking at the difference between the rich and the rest is to consider accumulated wealth. In the United States today, an elite one percent controls 40 percent of the nation's wealth, while the bottom 80 percent shares only seven percent. Wealth is so unfairly distributed in America that the wealthiest 400 individuals own more than the bottom 150,000,000 people.

To understand what has happened in the United States, we must look at the political system that has allowed—indeed encouraged—the redistribution of income and wealth from the working and middle classes to the upper class. The Dream realized by most Americans in the three decades following World War II was fueled by the high incomes and low taxes enjoyed by working people and small business owners and by the high taxes paid by large corporations and the wealthy.

The balance among classes was maintained by a compromise government, in which the working and middle classes were mostly represented by the Democratic Party and the wealthy and corporations by the Republican Party. Both parties realized the nation benefitted when people were healthy, well paid, well housed, and well educated. It was this compromise government that provided the Social Security Retirement and Disability system and Medicare for the elderly and disabled, that built the bridges and highways connecting the nation, and which set aside and maintained the national parks for the enjoyment and relaxation of the people.

Today, in the United States, the two-party system has become a political hoax perpetrated by the major corporations and the wealthy elite to convince the working and middle classes they continue to have representation in their government. Although the two parties may express differences on social matters, such as reproductive and marriage rights, they are in virtual lockstep on economic, environmental, security, and military matters.

Changing Course

The Republican Party has been driven to the extreme far right and into a state of uncompromising obstruction by its radical wing, and the Democratic Party has been moved right of center by its neo-liberal wing. Noam Chomsky—a traditional liberal—says the United States has only the Business Party, with two factions called Democrats and Republicans. Ron Paul—a traditional libertarian—argues there is essentially no difference between one administration and another, no matter what the platform. Denial is dangerous, and American voters have to face the truth: there is but one political party in the United States, with two factions—just as in China.

Empowered by Supreme Court decisions conferring constitutional rights on corporations, the local, state, and federal governments of the United States are being manipulated by corporations and the wealthy elite who control them. There is little ordinary working people and small-business owners can do about it, and their votes are becoming worthless.

Moreover, just as the one-party dictatorship in China provides a nutrient broth for the growth of corruption, the same situation occurs in the United States. In both places, bribes for political decisions and lucrative contracts can be disguised as campaign contributions and consulting fees, or laundered through friends and relatives. In both countries, the people's representatives are bought and paid for by entities that have different interests than the people, and representatives and their relatives get rich in the bargain.

The danger is not so much that China will continue with its one-party dictatorship, but that the United States will continue to further coalesce into a one-party system that will look to China as a model for the corporate success of autocratic political decision making. The neo-conservatives won the battle in China after Tiananmen Square, and the neo-cons of the United States continue to mimic them—as they increasingly seek to impose a repressive regime on Americans.

Just as the state-controlled media fails to provide the Chinese people with truthful and accurate information about the operations of their government, the United States mainstream news media has come to be almost entirely dominated by the very same corporations that have seized control of the government.

People in both countries, who are seeking truthful and factual information, are turning to the Internet and online social media. In both countries, the governments control, manipulate, and distort the flow of information, while subjecting those who use electronic communications to intensive surveillance.

Communism is not the Same as Socialism, and Capitalism is not the Same as Free Enterprise

The Chinese Communist Party maintains it must preserve its dictatorial control of the government and economy for the next hundred years or so, as the nation is guided through its socialism stage toward the goal of an ideal communist state. To the extent it ever did, the Party no longer provides retirement and health care for ordinary Chinese people. Instead, the people now contribute to a social security and a subsidized health insurance system, which offers far fewer benefits than those provided by the developed nations in the West, including the United States.

By the measure of what governments actually provide for the social well-being of its citizens, Western nations, particularly the Scandinavian countries, are much more socialistic than China, or any of the other remaining communist countries. Indeed, the nation of India, which has almost as many people as China, defines itself as a socialist nation in its constitution. Giving lie to the Communist Party assertion that its single-party dictatorship is required to manage a population in excess of one billion, India has a multitude of parties, including two different brands of communism. Moreover, the Quality of Life Index in India is three times that of China.

Because of the Marxism-Leninism dialectic, the word socialism has come to have a negative connotation in the United States, as it has been associated with the failure of communism. The word has a far richer meaning, however, and it does not have a good synonym. Socialism can and should mean that a truly representative government is oriented to the society that elects if. As such, it should provide the people what they really want and need: health care for their families, education for their children, a secure retirement and disability system, sensible regulation of the economy and environment, and a fair system of justice.

Communism, where the means of production are owned and operated by the state, has been conclusively proven a complete failure in every country trying it, including China. Rather than admitting its failure, the Chinese Communist Party insists that China is still passing through the "primary stage of socialism," but now requires the profits produced by capitalism to continue on to pure communism. This is utter nonsense, and it is time for productive self-criticism.

The Chinese people have the ability to think for themselves, and they should be able to determine if they would like to enjoy the fruits of real socialism and make it work for themselves. They do not have to continue struggling toward an ideal communist utopia under the dictatorship of the Chinese Communist Party. Along with Americans, the Chinese people deserve a truly representative government that cares for their needs and aspirations.

Just as communism does not mean the same thing as socialism, capitalism does not mean the same thing as free enterprise. Unregulated capitalism is a psychotic economic system, which is without empathy for the rights and needs of workers who labor to produce profits. A corporation does not and cannot have a conscience. Indeed, in its defined mission of seeking the greatest profit, or return, on its investment, a care or concern for others is counterproductive. A worker's health, injury, or death is just another cost to be factored into the equation. The well-being of consumers harmed by defective products, or other suffering caused by the pollution generated in the profit-making process is just another cost in the process of generating wealth.

Free enterprise is more than capitalism—much more. Freedom is required to make free enterprise work, which requires a balance in power between labor and capital. Each must have the freedom and opportunity to make choices in the pursuit of happiness.

American and Chinese workers, and the small business owners of both countries, do not presently have the freedom to make choices. Workers have little freedom in China because the dictatorship is increasingly under the control of the bureaucrats, technocrats, and corporate managers who dominate the Party's leadership. Workers have lost their freedom in America because their ability to organize and collectively bargain has been crushed, as their corporate employers have gained extraordinary political power to manipulate the laws and control the regulatory and judicial processes.

All Governments Have a Duty to Educate Their People and to Tell Them the Truth

One of the most significant achievements of the United States was the establishment of a comprehensive public school system, which provided 12 years of basic education for every student. Moreover, during the American Dream era, the states established a complex of public colleges and universities that made post-secondary and graduate studies accessible to the vast majority of working and middle-class families. All of this is being lost and destroyed in Corporate America by the imposition of the business model on education. Not only has mind-numbing testing been introduced throughout the system, even into the kindergartens, but neo-conservative forces are attempting to shift the entire public education system into alternative profit-driven "charter schools."

For those who are not fortunate enough to have been born into wealthy American families, a college education now requires the borrowing of substantial student loans. Repayment of these loans burden graduates throughout most of their productive years and cannot be discharged in bankruptcy. Even so, U.S. colleges and universities are graduating hundreds of thousands of smart and bright-eyed young people, for whom there are few job opportunities to repay the cost of their education.

Since establishing the People's Republic of China in 1949, education of the masses by the Communist Party has had varying degrees of success. The two most disastrous reversals came during the Great Leap Forward and the Cultural Revolution, which wiped out many gains, but since the death of Mao, there has been steady progress. Today, Chinese students can be educated at government expense from elementary through graduate school, and the government reports 99.7 percent of the student population has received the minimum nine years of basic education.

There are now more than 2,000 private and public colleges and universities in China, with an enrollment of more than six million students. Entrance standards are highest for the public schools, ten of which have been designated to receive extra government funding in order to become "world-class" institutions. Acceptance at all schools is determined by entrance examination scores, and 9.39 million students took the exam in June 2014.

Approximately 20 percent of college-age young people in China are now receiving higher education; however, cheating is widespread, and rote memorization interferes with the development of critical thinking skills.

It is clear from all of this that the citizens of both the United States and China presently have the minimum education necessary to actively participate in deciding for themselves the direction they want their governments to move. Even so, all young people need to have solid educational foundations in civics and the principles of self-government. Everyone deserves accurate and truthful information about critical political, economic, and environmental issues.

The proper role of government in a functioning representative democracy is to comprehensively research important political issues and to present alternative solutions to the people to decide the policies they want their government to follow. In neither the United States nor China is the government fulfilling that duty. In fact, both conceal and distort the truths they fear would cause their citizens to mistrust and criticize their governments.

Informed Voters Must Make Their Own Policy

The Republic of China in Taiwan has held several referenda in accordance with its Constitution of 1947, but the People's Republic of China has never trusted its people to collectively vote on any political or economic policy issue, including their own constitution.

Individual American states occasionally allow their people to vote on various initiatives, propositions, and state constitutional amendments, but the federal government has never held a national vote on any issue. In general, the experience of the states has taught that the initiative process is not the best way to enact *laws*, which should be left to the more deliberative legislative process.

The formulation of *policy* is, however, an entirely different matter. Unlike laws, which are necessarily rigorous, and in which every exception has to be carefully defined, policies are broad, general guidelines, with more philosophical implications. For example, the people are quite capable of answering a question about whether they want their government to provide them with comprehensive national health care, instead of subsidized mandatory health insurance. Exactly how such a program should be set up, implemented, and funded are matters best left to elected legislators and executives to work out.

Political policies are secretly formulated in China by the Communist Party leadership and enshrined in the constitution at Party Congresses. They are presented to the people through the state-controlled media and disseminated through the Party bureaucracy. Examples are Xi's China Dream, Hu's Harmonious Society, and Jiang's Three Represents.

The process in the United States is a little different, but no better. Political policies are developed by individual candidates and/or confirmed as platforms at political party conventions. The policies and platforms become something like slogans in an advertising campaign to sell a particular product. The people are forced to select between the policies of opposing candidates and/or party platforms at election time. The problem is that, once elected, the representatives freely ignore what they promised to do to get elected, and they consistently take action contrary to the real needs and wishes of those who elected them.

One of the best examples of a policy referendum occurred in 2004, when the voters of the Republic of China on Taiwan were asked two questions about relations with the People's Republic of China on the mainland:

Changing Course

1. The People of Taiwan demand that the Taiwan Strait issue be resolved through peaceful means. Should Communist China refuse to withdraw the missiles it has targeted at Taiwan and to openly renounce the use of force against us, would you agree that the Government should acquire more advanced anti-missile weapons to strengthen Taiwan's self-defense capabilities?
2. Would you agree that our Government should engage in negotiation with Communist China on the establishment of a "peace and stability" framework for cross-strait interactions in order to build consensus and for the welfare of the peoples on both sides?

Beijing considered the vote to be a step toward an independent Taiwan and opposed the referendum. An alliance of Taiwanese parties, including the Kuomintang, called for a boycott believing the vote was unnecessary in their continuing desire to unite all of China. The boycott was successful, with less than a 50 percent turnout, but more than 90 percent of those who did vote answered both questions in the affirmative.

How would the mainland Chinese people answer this question: "Should the dictatorship of the Chinese Communist Party continue?" It is unlikely such a referendum would be allowed, but other questions less destructive of the Party's monopoly of power might pave the way for the ultimate question.

The policies already adopted by the Communist Party and enshrined in the constitution provide a basis for a national movement to allow the Chinese people to vote in policy referenda. Mao himself thought:

To link oneself with the masses, one must act in accordance with the needs and wishes of the masses. All work done for the masses must start from their needs and not from the desire or any individual, however well-intentioned.

Jiang's Three Represents recognizes "the fundamental interests of the overwhelming majority of the Chinese People." Xi's urging young people to "contribute their wisdom and energy to the realization of the Chinese Dream" certainly provides the encouragement of a youth-led, Internet-based movement with a clearly defined political focus: "Let us vote for ourselves!"

Equally important, American voters should be able to decide for themselves if they want to continue supporting a defense budget that exceeds the combined military budgets of China, Russia, United Kingdom, France, Japan, Saudi Arabia, India, Germany, India, and Brazil. Do the people of the United States really want to have their sons and daughters in the military to be based in more than 150 countries around the world?

Voting is an Inherent Human Right

Most modern governments, including China and the United States, are putative republics, which means the people are supposed to be represented in government. In a pure democracy (or ideal communism), everyone would vote on each and every issue, every time. What chaos would ensue!

Governments in the West are generally representative democracies, in which qualified voters select among candidates proposed by multiple parties. In the United States, there are subtle surface differences between the candidates of the various parties, and they each have their individual selling points; however, most of the candidates at the state and federal levels share similar views on the economy, military, security, and environment. These views are more aligned with the expectations and demands of the corporations and wealthy elite that pay for the campaigns, than the needs and desires of the people who cast the votes.

In the United States, elections are using computerized voting machines, on which the names of candidates are flashed on screens, and voters press buttons to indicate their choices. These computers can be easily hacked and manipulated, and paper ballots are increasingly rare.

There is, in fact, no federal constitutional right to vote in the United States, and various states have made it difficult or impossible for many people to vote. Acting in the absence of any real evidence of election fraud, voter identification laws prevent voters, without driver's licenses or other acceptable identification, from voting. These laws primarily disenfranchise students, the poor, and the elderly. In addition, the intentional reduction in the number of available and convenient polling places at certain locations, including college campuses, result in lower voter turnouts.

The proposed United States Voters' Rights Amendment (USVRA) is a voters' bill of rights that would guarantee the right of voters to cast *effective* ballots by:

- defining equal rights for women;
- maximizing voter participation and prohibiting the suppression of voting;
- eliminating corporate personhood and controlling political contributions;
- public funding of elections and limiting campaigns;
- increasing congressional representation;
- voting holidays and paper ballots;
- improving political education and public information;
- voters deciding policy issues;
- eliminating the Electoral College; and
- curtailing lobbying and prohibiting conflicts of interest.

In the People's Republic of China, local units of the Chinese Communist Party screen and propose candidates for the National People's Congress and the Chinese People's Political Consultative Conference, which are held in March of each year in Beijing. Proposed candidates are then reviewed at each succeeding higher level of the Communist Party, up through regions and provinces, until decisions comes down from the top, naming the 5,000 selected delegates. Once the delegates arrive in Beijing, they are presented with thousands of motions, the contents of which are never made public. Virtually all motions are unanimously approved by the delegates.

Upon nomination by the Presidium of the People's Congress, delegates are allowed to vote approval or disapproval of single candidates to various high offices, including President, Vice President, Chairman of the Central Military Commission and President of the Supreme People's Court. While these nominations are always approved, there have been occasions when the names of alternates have been written in.

There has been some freeing up of elections at the village level, but the average Chinese citizen never gets to see a ballot, much less vote. In theory, representatives at each level are selected at lower levels, but, in practice, it is just the opposite. Candidates are vetted and approved at higher levels, and candidate selections are imposed downward from the top.

The very essence of democracy is voting, and the foundation of representative government is having a choice of candidates with differing points of view. The most effective manner of voting is for voters to secretly handwrite their decisions and choices on durable paper ballots, which can then be carefully hand counted and recounted if necessary.

Voting, as a physical act that can be visibly demonstrated, is the only nonviolent power individuals can actually grasp in their hands against the tyranny of unrepresentative government! If voters are handed a ballot listing nominees that do not represent the voters' views, they have a moral duty to demonstrate their power and literacy by carefully writing in the name of any person they choose, including their own.

Voters presented with computerized machines can demand a paper ballot on which to write in their choice. If their demand is refused, voters can simply deposit a paper ballot of their own creation. Whether or not the vote is ever counted, the physical act of a vote of conscience is a forceful demonstration of individual power.

In jurisdictions where there are no actual elections, voters can still demonstrate their personal political power by holding their own unsanctioned elections, casting carefully-considered paper ballots, and reporting the results.

If voters are physically blocked from conducting their own elections, they can vote on the Internet and via social media, they can vote on posters pasted on walls, or in dozens of other imaginative and creative ways. Determined voters cannot be prevented from demonstrating their votes of conscience. As a nonviolent act, the power of demonstrative voting in securing a peaceful society is far superior to, and much more effective than, violence.

The right to cast an effective vote on matters of concern, including representation, is an inherent human right. It may be the most important right, because without real voting power, all other rights, including free speech and assembly, can be forfeited.

Confucius was speaking for everyone when he said the people have the right to rebel against an unjust ruler. When a ruler denies the right of some, or all of the people, to cast effective votes, the rule is inherently unjust, and the people have to chose the most creative and effective way to rebel. In his commentary on Confucius, Mencius reiterated that humans are inherently good.

In the Declaration of Independence, the founders of the United States expressed the philosophy that government is responsible to and for the people:

> Governments are instituted among Men, deriving their just powers from the consent of the governed. That whenever any Form of Government becomes destructive of these ends, it is the Right of the People to alter or to abolish it, and to institute new Government, laying its foundation on such principles and organizing its powers in such form, as to them shall seem most likely to effect their Safety and Happiness.

These principles are still valid, and ordinary people in every nation are now more morally, mentally, and emotionally capable of self-government than ever before in history.

The dynamic of voting is the only power left in the hands of individual citizens, which can be demonstrated without the consent of party leaders or government authorities. The empowerment of the voting experience is the key to freedom!

The Power and Payoff of Freedom

Even though it is under attack by conservative and fundamentalist forces, there is a high level of intellectual freedom in the United States, which has allowed it to develop and generate leading-edge ideas, inventions, and solutions in science, medicine, industry, and the arts. Implementation of greater voting freedoms would certainly improve the intellectual productivity of Americans, but it is in China where the greatest gains could be achieved.

The Chinese people have demonstrated great inner resources by their ability to repeatedly recover from the tragedies they have suffered in the last 150 years. Commencing with the corporate colonization of China by Western imperialist powers, the ravages of revolutions and wars, the slaughter of millions by Mao Zedong, and the crushing limitations of institutional totalitarianism, the people of China have been tested beyond endurance. Yet, they have survived and are prepared to achieve even greater accomplishments—if given the chance.

The leaders of the Chinese Communist Party may question the value of surrendering their dictatorial control of China and its government. But, in considering the question, they must carefully analyze how much of China's productive power is dependent on the intellectual work produced in Western nations with greater individual freedom. For example, while China exports millions of computers and other electronic devices each year, they are mostly controlled by integrated circuits and processors designed and produced in other countries.

The Communist Party leadership must calculate how much the suppression of intellectual freedom is costing China today and how much it is limiting future development. The Party must balance the weaker risk of domestic instability with the powerful surge of strength that will result from the abdication of its dictatorship.

If we recall, the attempt by an enlightened emperor in the last days of the Manchurian Qing dynasty to reform the government into a democratic constitutional monarchy was slapped down by conservative leaders on his Council. Considering that the dynasty fell 12 years later in the

Republican Revolution, there may be some lessons there for the present Communist Party leadership. It would seem much more advantageous for the Party to initiate actual democratic changes, rather than to just talk about them. Sooner, rather than later, is the best time to change course when a ship is heading for the rocks.

Deng Xiaoping, in his later years, endorsed the idea that the social experience of the people was the only way to evaluate the truth of a doctrine. He concluded Marxism had to be constantly reinterpreted based on experience and practice. This kind of thinking was certainly the basis for China's adoption of capitalist market principles, and it could be the justification and motivation for the Party to voluntarily relinquish its dictatorship.

In the final analysis, the Party leadership must come to trust the great latent power of the Chinese people more than they trust their own authoritarian control. With freedom, China may once again show the world what can only be presently imagined and is yet to be invented.

Just as freedom must be expanded in China, if it is to achieve its potential, the present curtailment of freedom in the United States must be reversed, if it is to retain its creativity. Conservatives and religious fundamentalists have imposed regressive policies on government programs and spending in the U.S. that have interfered with scientific and economic progress. In every case, these policies represent minority positions, albeit vocal and well funded ones.

The majority must exercise its remaining freedoms to ensure that the voices of collective reason prevail. Enactment of the United States Voters' Rights Amendment would do much to correct the imbalance of political power in America and would allow its people to take control of their government and to be less threatening to the people of other nations.

A Peaceful Pacific Community

Throughout most of its four-thousand-year history, China was content to live within its borders and behind its Great Wall and ocean shoreline.

An Essential History of China

It expected and received respect from its neighboring countries—from whom it received tribute and returned gifts of greater value. During the greatest extent of its ocean explorations, the mighty ships of the Ming dynasty were primarily designed to engage in trade and diplomacy. They transported ambassadors from other countries to and from China in great comfort. With its ability to raise vast armies and build mighty ships, and to equip them with the superior technologies of the era, China could have conquered all of human civilization. It choose not to do so, because it already had what it wanted and needed.

The world has changed in that China now requires raw materials from around the world to feed its industrial machines, and its people want to share in the "dreams" of developed nations, but the essential psychology of the Chinese culture remains unchanged. China wants to be a responsible power, and it mainly seeks to be safe within its borders and to solve its own internal problems in its own way and in its own time.

Seeing itself as the world's only superpower, the United States maintains hundreds of foreign military bases around the world. China has none. The United States spends more than $640 billion on its military each year, which is more than the next eight nations combined. At number two position, China's military budget is $118 billion. Relying on its military to solve its international problems, the United States' policy is reminiscent of the proverb: "If all you have is a hammer, everything looks like a nail."

The one thing that should be clear to all geopolitical decision makers concerned with China is that *it will not be contained*. China must be dealt with in terms of the realities of its existence. What then, is the best way to go about securing peace and avoiding another devastating war in the Pacific?

The Japanese post-war constitution promises to achieve an international peace based on justice and order, rather than belligerency and war. Perhaps we can start there in seeking a peaceful solution to the problems of the Pacific.

Rather than acting belligerently, as China takes its legitimate place among the major powers of the world, the United States should organize a conference of all nations bordering the Pacific Ocean, including China's immediate neighbors of North and South Korea, Russia, Japan, the Philippines, and Vietnam, plus Indonesia, Singapore, India, the nations of the middle east and eastern Africa, Australia, New Zealand, South and Central America, Mexico, and Canada.

The agenda might seek agreement by all Pacific nations to:

- respect existing borders;
- avoid belligerency and seek mediation of all territorial and trade disputes;
- judiciously serve, if randomly selected, on mediation panels composed of Pacific nations;
- deploy defensive, rather than offensive military forces;
- avoid the trade of military weapons;
- cooperate in the suppression of piracy;
- acknowledge the right of all Pacific nations to exist and to trade in peace;
- allow each nation to solve its own internal problems; and
- work toward a form of representative government that best meets the social needs and political rights of their own people.

This is a Pacific Dream, and the young people of the Pacific nations have the ability, flexibility, and incentive to make it come true. The rest of us are too old and set in our ways. We can only rely on the limited wisdom we have gained from our life's experiences to suggest a way forward. Our children have to walk the path into the future without us. Let us do all we can to prepare them for the journey and to make it as safe, peaceful, and interesting as possible.

Making History

It is one thing to read history, which can be quite fascinating, as well as informative. All one has to do is pick up a book and concentrate on the written word. It is quite another thing to actually make history—as the opportunities to do so are rare indeed.

The people of China and the United States can make history. They can create the images for this evening's television news and they can dictate the headlines of tomorrow's newspapers. Or, they can continue to live with repression, making accommodations with their consciences, and enjoying what little comfort is allowed to them by the forces of greed.

Young people, everywhere, have the duty to peacefully take action to seize their freedom, which is the inherent right of all humans. They have the education, incentive, and the power to do so, and they have the motivation. They are the ones who will have to breath the air, drink the water, and labor under repression. Their survival is at stake.

We, who have lived past our youth, have learned the limitations of life. Hopefully, we have also achieved the wisdom to work with others to surmount the barriers to progress and to see beyond our limited vision. Our duty is to educate, encourage, support, and prepare our children for their voyage into a future that is beyond our ability to perceive.

Epilogue

Democracy in Hong Kong

As *An Essential History of China* was being written in September 2014, student demonstrations about voting rights began to take place in Hong Kong. Nothing could be more relevant to the premise of this book, so let's briefly review the background, issues, progress, and consequences of the protests.

The United Kingdom and the Republic of China were allies during World War II. At the end of the war, Hong Kong was a British Crown Colony, as provided for under existing treaties. English control of the colony had continued uninterrupted after the Republic of China retreated to Taiwan in 1949 and the People's Republic of China was established on the mainland.

Hong Kong was entirely dependent on the mainland for food and water, but Mao Zedong decided to leave Hong Kong intact—as it was a source of hard currency and a pipeline for embargoed goods and technology.

During the Cultural Revolution, Mao tried to stir up labor disputes in Hong Kong by authorizing a series of bombings and encouraging workers to kill police officers. Public opinion turned against the rioters, and the Hong Kong police arrested the bombers.

Hong Kong Island was ceded in perpetuity to England, but its lease of the New Territories of Hong Kong was set to expire in 1997. Following the independence of India, England began to nudge all of its colonies toward freedom and democracy. The Hong Kong leadership considered allowing popular elections, but abandoned the idea when the Chinese Communist Party threatened to forcefully liberate Hong Kong.

As the date for expiration of the lease approached, Chris Patten, the last Governor of Hong Kong, ignored Beijing's threats and allowed voters to directly elect 30 members of a 60-member Legislative Council. He said, "People in Hong Kong are perfectly capable of taking a greater share in managing their own affairs in a way that is responsible, mature, restrained, [and] sensible."

England and the People's Republic of China engaged in negotiations leading to a Joint Declaration in 1984, which established the terms under which England would surrender all of its rights in Hong Kong to China in 1997. China announced its policy of "one country, two systems." In 1993, the Director of the Hong Kong and Macau Affairs Office of China's State Council stated, "How Hong Kong develops democracy in the future is a matter entirely within the sphere of Hong Kong's autonomy, and the central government cannot intervene."

In preparation for the turnover, and in conformance with the Joint Declaration, the Chinese government drafted the Hong Kong Basic Law as a constitution to govern Hong Kong until 2047. The people of Hong Kong were consulted and participated in the formation of the Law, under which China is supreme in the areas of foreign relations and military defense. In most other respects, Hong Kong retained a high degree of autonomy as a "Special Administrative Region of China."

Hong Kong's special status included maintenance of the English Common Law system under an independent judiciary, its own flag and currency, independent membership in world trade and financial organizations, and multi-party election of representatives to its Legislative Council.

The Basic Law allows voters to directly elect 35 members of the 70-member legislative council, while the other 35 members are elected by a smaller group of electors, which include corporate bodies and certain specified functional sectors. The Chief Executive presides over the Council.

In the past, chief executive candidates, including the incumbent, were vetted by an elite committee of 1,200 prominent Hong Kong residents, most of whom supported the People's Republic of China. The Chief Executive has been appointed by the central government in Beijing, but will be elected by Hong Kong voters in 2017. Currently, the primary issue is whether an elite committee should continue to screen candidates for the office, or should the voters nominate their own candidates.

Under its terms, the governing Basic Law is subject to interpretation and amendment by the Standing Committee of China's National People's Congress and the Congress itself.

In 2003, Beijing's attempt to impose new security laws on Hong Kong was opposed by a gathering of more than 500,000 people. The laws were withdrawn, and the chief executive was forced to resign.

The current controversy stems from a provision of the Basic Law which guarantees the selection of the chief executive and all members of the Legislative Council by way of "universal suffrage." Support of universal suffrage primarily comes from a pan-democracy political faction, whose delegates usually receive around 60 percent of the popular vote in Hong Kong elections.

In 2007, the Chief Executive published a Green Paper on Constitutional Development, which was submitted to the National Congress. The decision was that the chief executive could be elected by universal suffrage in 2017, and thereafter, all members of the Legislative Council could be elected by universal suffrage.

The current Hong Kong voting controversy involves both legal and political matters. There is a dispute about the legal meaning of universal suffrage and the standard by which it is to be decided. The Chinese Communist Party believes the National Congress has the authority under the Basic Law to interpret the meaning of suffrage, while the Hong Kong pan-democracy faction urges that international standards prevail. An additional legal problem is that England itself did not apply the Universal Covenant of Civil and Political Rights for universal suffrage to Hong Kong prior to the turnover.

Reflecting the international standard, the United Nations Human Rights Committee has informed China that universal suffrage includes the right to nominate candidates, as well as the right to vote for them.

Politically, the Communist Party wants Hong Kong to follow the same nominating process used in the remainder of China, where the Party nominates its own members for all offices. Naturally, Beijing fears that allowing Hong Kong voters to actually nominate their own candidates might infect people on the mainland with the disease of real democracy, leading to a demand for multiple political parties and the demise of the Communist Party dictatorship.

At the same time, the central government recognizes the massive role the Hong Kong business and financial institutions play in China's economy, which has shifted from state subsidies to reliance on banking investments. The People's Republic of China relies on the support of the conservative Hong Kong business and financial community, which, in turn, benefits from the current pro-capitalist policies of the Communist Party.

Beijing maintains its oversight of Hong Kong through its Central Liaison Office. The Office owns a luxurious villa complex just over the border in Shenzhen province, from which it monitors and seeks to control events in Hong Kong.

Leung Chun-ying, the current Chief Executive of Hong Kong, established a Task Force on Constitutional Development in October 2013 to engage in a five-month period of public consultation. Issues included the size of the Council, the electoral base of the functional constituency, the number of geographical constituencies, and the number of seats assigned to each. A Consultation Report was issued in July 2014 and submitted to the National Congress.

A preemptive White Paper issued by Beijing the previous month made clear it has "comprehensive jurisdiction" over Hong Kong. Any autonomy is subject to authorization, and only "patriots" will be allowed to hold key posts in Hong Kong. Essentially, the White Paper changed the Party's "one country two systems" policy. Hong Kong's delegate to the National Congress was quoted as saying, "The White Paper serves to clear out any confusion that people in Hong Kong may have about one country two systems."

Democracy in Hong Kong

A few weeks later, the pan-democracy movement responded with the Public Opinion Program, which was conducted by the University of Hong Kong. The unofficial computerized referendum gave Hong Kong voters three options for selecting their next chief executive, all of which allowed the public to nominate candidates. As soon as the polls opened, referendum computers were struck by an unrelenting massive cyber attack. Overcoming the assault, 1.8 million Hong Kong voters, of the 3.5 million registered, exercised their franchise and expressed their choices through the Internet.

On August 31, 2014, the National Congress issued its ruling regarding universal suffrage. Emphasizing patriotism as a condition, the decision was that the chief executive must be a person "who loves the Country and loves Hong Kong." Implementation of this ruling requires screening to ensure the purity of each candidate's love. Screening is to be performed by a blue ribbon, 1,200-member, nominating committee consisting of central government loyalists, which will nominate two or three candidates. Once elected, the chief executive will be appointed by Beijing.

While a majority of the 7.2 million people of Hong Kong responded with dismay to the Congressional decision, it was their young people who took to the streets in protest. Organized by the Hong Kong Federation of Students and the Scholarism organization, protests commenced on September 22, 2014, when a large group occupied the forecourt of the Central Government Complex. They were forcibly removed the next day, but they launched a civil disobedience campaign.

Protesters blocked the main east and west downtown traffic routes on September 28, but were once again removed by force, including the use of tear gas. Primarily composed of students—who boycotted classes—the protesters began to use umbrellas as a protection against tear gas and a symbol of resistance. The names of Occupy Central and the Umbrella Revolution were used to describe the protests. The primary and continuing demand was for free and fair elections, and the protesters began to call for Leung's resignation.

Commencing on October 2, the demonstrators occupied the streets surrounding the Central Government Headquarters and began to inspect shipments into the facility to ensure weapons and tear gas were not being brought in. Violence was initiated against protesters in the surrounding areas by anti-occupy activists—assisted by Triad criminal gang members. The police made some arrests, but there were complaints they were not protecting the protesters from physical assaults.

Hong Kong authorities promised to talk with the demonstrators, and university officials and liberal politicians urged the young people to leave the streets for their own protection. The number of occupiers began to decline, but when the government canceled a meeting with students, thousands of protesters gathered on October 11 and 12. Hundreds of tents were pitched, blocking a main traffic artery, and food, water, and medical supplies were assembled.

Police officers began to remove barricades to open up the streets to traffic, and masked reactionaries began to cut down barricades and attack occupiers. Demonstrators quickly reinstalled barriers and blocked traffic on yet another major street. The police responded with batons and pepper spray to clear the roadway. A television news clip documenting a four-minute video of police officers beating an occupier went viral on the Internet and was seen around the world. Journalists were also treated harshly by the police.

After almost a month of daily protests, the police dismantled barricades, removed tents from the main encampment and drove most of the demonstrators from the streets. The demonstrators did not surrender. A thousand of them put on helmets and goggles, picked up their umbrellas, and rushed the police lines, driving the police back. They were confronted with pepper spray and batons, but they held their own and continued to occupy the streets in downtown Hong Kong.

The demonstrators primarily occupied "Umbrella Plaza" in the Admiralty area, where students gathered for speeches, entertainment, and make-shift classes. Older protesters, including white- and blue-collar workers, gathered in the Mong Kok area.

The Chief Executive finally agreed to talk with student representatives and designated his assistant to conduct the negotiations. During the televised dialogue on October 21, the students dressed in T-shirts emblazoned with Freedom Now! sat across from government representatives wearing business suits. Students repeated their demands for universal suffrage, and the officials urged them to accept a token concession as a start toward greater democracy. The government stated it would consider sending a supplementary report to Beijing, documenting concerns of the protesters. There was no agreement.

During an interview with Western journalists, Chief Executive Leung revealed another aspect of the political issues involved in universal suffrage. He said the chief executive could not be chosen in open elections because it would risk giving poor voters a dominant voice in government. He said, "if it's entirely a numbers game and numeric representation, then obviously you would be talking to half of the people in Hong Kong who earn less than $1,800 a month."

Student protestors massed around the stately Government House where Leung lives and shouted "Shame on you." The police did not interfere with their peaceful protest.

In dealing with the Hong Kong democracy protests, the Communist Party leadership confronted institutional memories of two events. First, they had a real fear of losing control of the country—as happened during the Cultural Revolution. Second, they remembered and wanted to avoid the international and universal condemnation of the violent manner in which the leadership responded to the student demonstrations in Tiananmen Square.

As the days went by and the protesters did not go away, Hong Kong officials gathered each morning at the Bauhinia Villa in Shenzhen to report on the situation to their Beijing masters and to receive instructions on how to proceed. The Central Liaison Office briefed President Xi at least once a day.

It was a difficult balancing act that placed an extraordinary burden on the Hong Kong 28,000-member police force to clear the protesters—but to do so in a way that did not result in images of violence. As time passed, nerves on both sides of the barricades become frayed and the morale of both the police and protesters suffered.

For more than two months, the students demonstrated the sincerity of their belief in the cause of universal suffrage and their willingness to suffer arrests and tear gassings, and the authorities mostly showed restraint. The authorities attempted to wait out the students and hoped that public pressure, their parents, and school officials would convince them to leave the streets and return to classes.

By the end of November 2014, only a few hundred protesters remained in tents at three sites. The demonstrations were finally ended by the use of a civil court process. The Hong Kong bus transportation company obtained a court order against the street blockages, which was enforced by court bailiffs, with the support of the police. Anyone who interfered with the court bailiffs, as they removed the barricades, tents, and other items, was arrested for violating the court order. In a further extension of the judicial solution, arrestees were prohibited from returning to specified locations, as a condition of being released on bail.

In a final demonstration of solidarity with the students, dozens of lawyers, lawmakers, and other leaders were arrested and carried away when they refused to leave the last of the major encampments.

Through the end of December 2014, protesters engaged in "shopping" demonstrations as they paraded on the sidewalks through the downtown area. Resurgent protests temporarily blocked roads and several dozen demonstrators submitted to arrests. By the new year, downtown Hong Kong was quiet—but it would never again be the same.

The students acted as the vanguard for the adult pan-democratic movement and organized labor. During the Cultural Revolution, Mao attempted to rally Hong Kong labor unions against the city's business and financial interests. In an ironic twist of fate, Mao's present successors used the business and financial elite of Hong Kong to keep its labor unions and other riffraff under control. One reason why the students took the lead in the democracy movement is the difference between being fined for participating in an unlawful assembly, and being locked up for life for committing treason against the state.

Democracy in Hong Kong

In August 2015, almost a year after the occupation events, two of the primary student leaders were arrested. Alex Chow, the leader of the Hong Kong Federation of Students and Joshua Wong, the leader of the Scholarism group, were charged with the crime of inciting and illegal assembly. Their prosecution is pending.

Irrespective of the outcome, the young people of Hong Kong have achieved a major victory. They have forced the minions of the most powerful political party in the world to sit down and listen to their demands, and they fixed the validity and reasonableness of those demands in the consciousness and conscience of the free world.

The United States Voters' Rights Amendment (USVRA)

Section 1.

The right of all citizens of the United States, who are eighteen years of age or older, to cast effective votes in political elections is inherent under this Constitution and shall not be denied or abridged by the United States or by any State.

Section 2.

Equality of rights under the law shall not be denied or abridged by the United States or by any State on account of sex.

Section 3.

The States shall ensure that all citizens who are eligible to vote are registered to vote.

In balancing the public benefit of maximum voter participation with the prevention of voting fraud, Congress and the States shall not impose any unjustifiable restriction on registration or voting by citizens.

The intentional suppression of voting is hereby prohibited and, in addition to any other penalty imposed by law, any person convicted of the intentional suppression of voting shall be ineligible for public office for a period of five years following such conviction.

Section 4.

The rights protected by the Constitution of the United States are the rights of natural persons only.

Artificial entities established by the laws of any State, the United States, or any foreign state shall have no rights under this Constitution and are subject to regulation by the People, through Federal, State, or local law.

The privileges of artificial entities shall be determined by the People, through Federal, State, or local law, and shall not be construed to be inherent or inalienable.

SECTION 5.

Federal, State and local government shall regulate, limit, or prohibit contributions and expenditures, to ensure that all citizens, regardless of their economic status, have access to the political process, and that no person gains, as a result of their money, substantially more access or ability to influence in any way the election of any candidate for public office or any ballot measure.

Federal, State and local government shall require that any permissible contributions and expenditures be publicly disclosed.

The judiciary shall not construe the spending of money to influence elections to be speech under the First Amendment.

SECTION 6.

Nothing contained in this article shall be construed to abridge the freedom of the press, which includes electronic and digital publication.

SECTION 7.

In balancing the public benefits of corruption-free elections with allowing candidates to accept private campaign contributions, Congress and the States shall favor public financing over private contributions.

Broadcasters using the public airwaves shall provide free airtime for political campaign programming; ensure controversial issues of public importance are presented in an honest, equitable and balanced manner; and provide equal time to opposing candidates and political points of view.

No campaign for elective public office, including receipt of campaign contributions, shall commence prior to six months before such election.

The United States Voters' Rights Amendment (USVRA)

Section 8.

Election districts represented by members of Congress, or by members of any State legislative body, shall be compact and composed of contiguous territory. The State shall have the burden of justifying any departures from this requirement by reference to neutral criteria such as natural, political, or historical boundaries or demographic changes. Enhancing or preserving the power of any political party or individual shall not be such a neutral criterion.

Congress shall apportion the number of representatives according to the decennial census to ensure the representation of a maximum of 250,000 Persons in each district.

Section 9.

It shall be a primary function of the government to ensure that the People are supplied with truthful, unbiased, objective, and timely information regarding the political, economic, environmental, financial, and social issues that affect them, and that all students are educated in the nature and responsibilities of representative democracy.

The University of the United States shall be established to incorporate all federal service academies and to provide education on the nature and responsibilities of representative democracy, the meaning of freedom, and the appropriate limitations on the use of coercion and force.

Section 10.

During the calendar year preceding a presidential election, Congress shall solicit public comment regarding the political issues that most concern the People.

Prior to the end of the calendar year preceding a presidential election, Congress shall adopt a joint resolution articulating questions regarding the twelve most critical policy issues to be addressed by the next president and Congress.

Failure of Congress to adopt such a joint resolution prior to the end of such calendar year shall result in the disqualification of all sitting members of Congress to be eligible for reelection.

SECTION 11.
Federal elections conducted every second year shall be held on a national voters' holiday, with full pay for all citizens who cast ballots.

Federal elections shall be conducted on uniform, hand-countable paper ballots and, for the presidential election, ballots shall include the twelve most critical policy questions articulated by Congress, each to be answered yes or no by the voters.

Paper ballots shall provide space allowing voters to handwrite in their choice for all elective federal offices, if they choose, and all such votes shall be counted.

SECTION 12.
Clauses Two and Three of Article Two, Section One and the Twelfth and Twenty-third articles of amendment to the Constitution of the United States are hereby repealed.

Clause Four of Article Two, Section One of the Constitution of the United States is amended to read as follows: "The Congress shall determine the dates of the primary and general elections of the president and vice president, which dates shall be the same throughout the United States. The presidential and vice presidential candidates receiving the most popular votes by all citizens of the United States shall be elected."

SECTION 13.
No person, having previously served as an official of the federal government, whether elected, appointed, employed, or serving in the military shall engage in any employment to advocate an interest or position to any Government official for a period of time following such service equal to the period of such service.

No person advocating an interest or position to any government official, whether or not for pay, shall offer or provide any campaign contribution, gifts, or things of value, including favors, services, travel, meals, entertainment, honoraria, and promises of future employment to such government official, nor shall such official accept any such proffering.

The United States Voters' Rights Amendment (USVRA)

Restrictions imposed on such persons by this section shall not be deemed to violate the rights of free speech or petition for redress.

SECTION 14.

No member of Congress, federal judge, or federal official shall vote, or rule on any matter in which such person or their spouse, domestic partner, child, or contributor of more than minor amounts of campaign funds has a financial, legal, or beneficial interest.

SECTION 15.

This article shall be inoperative unless it shall have been ratified as an amendment to the Constitution by conventions in the several States, as provided in the Constitution.

Delegates to State conventions to ratify this amendment shall be selected by special elections held within three months of its being proposed by Congress to the States. The voters in each congressional district in the several States shall elect one delegate. All delegate candidates shall affirm under oath when filing as a candidate whether they will vote yes or not for ratification of the proposed amendment, and their position shall be printed with their names on the special election ballot. Delegates shall not have the power to vote differently than their stated intention.

Conventions shall be held in the capitals of each State within three months of the election of delegates, with the chief justice of the highest court in the State chairing the convention. Tie votes by delegates shall be considered a vote for ratification.

The power of delegates convened pursuant to this section shall be restricted to voting yes or no for ratification of the proposed amendment. Such conventions shall not have the power to make changes to the proposed amendment or to consider other constitutional amendments.

The costs of ratification pursuant to this section shall be an expense of the federal government.

Sources

Inasmuch as the overriding objective of this writing effort was to produce a short, easily readable, and readily translatable book, footnotes and embedded notes were not included. They would slow down the reader, without necessarily adding to the information presented. Instead, the sources relied on in preparing each portion of the book are noted and acknowledged below. The author is indebted to these publications, those who authored them, and the society which has made them so readily available. In particular, the Asian Pacific Resource Center of the Los Angeles County Library, serving a Chinese-American population of more than 400,000 County residents, was extremely helpful.

Setting

Fairbank, John King, *China: A New History* (The Belnap Press of Harvard University Press, 1992). This was the last book written by Professor Fairbank, who was the Director of the East Asian Research Center at Harvard University, prior to his death in 1991. Fairbank's contribution was the most valuable in the preparation of this work. Readers interested in a more comprehensive history of China, combined with an intelligent discussion of that history, are well advised to start with Fairbank's book.

Part One - Four Thousand Years of Dynastic Rule
Ancient China

Fairbank, *op. cit.*

Feitman, Rachel, "These Ancient Chinese Teeth Could Rewrite Human History," *The Washington Post*, October 15, 2015.

Keay, John, *A History of China*, (Basic Books, 2009) Mr. Keay is an British author who has written a number of popular histories, including this one. A substantial effort, it was one of three primary sources which were found to be of great value in preparing this work.

Roberts, John A.G., *A Concise History of China* (Harvard University Press, Second Edition, 2006). Professor Roberts is the Principal Lecturer in History at the University of Huddersfield in the UK. Readers seeking a brief (300 pages), but well-written history of China should obtain this book, as it too was invaluable in the preparation of this work.

If Professor Roberts' book was the skeleton of the present work, Professor Fairbank's was the sinew that held it together and Mr. Keay added flesh. Roberts laid out what happened, Fairbanks taught how and why it happened, and Keay made it into a good story.

Schafer, Edward H., *Ancient China* (Time-Life Books, 1967).

Zimmer, Carl, "Man's Genome From 45,000 Years Ago Is Reconstructed," *The New York Times*, October 22, 2014.

EARLY DYNASTIES

Fairbank, *op. cit.*

Keay, *op. cit.*

Man, John, *The Terra Cotta Army: China's First Emperor and the Birth of a Nation*, (Da Capo Press, 2009).

Roberts, *op. cit.*

THE FIRST EMPEROR

Fairbank, *op. cit.*

Hardy, Grant and Anne Behnke Kinney, *The Establishment of the Han Empire and Imperial China*, (Greenwood Press, 2005).

Keay, *op. cit.*

LaFleur, Robert André, *China: A Global Studies Handbook*, (ABC CLIO, 2003).

Sources

Man, *op. cit.*
Roberts, *op. cit.*

THE HAN AND THE PERIOD OF DISUNION
Fairbank, *op. cit.*
Hardy and Kinney, *op. cit.*
Hook, Brian, Gen. Ed., *The Cambridge Encyclopedia of China*, (Cambridge University Press, 1982).
Keay, *op. cit.*
Roberts, *op. cit.*

THE SUI AND THE GRAND CANAL
Fairbank, *op. cit.*
Keay, *op. cit.*
Roberts, *op. cit.*
Wright, Arthur F., *The Sui Dynasty: The Unification of China, A.D. 581-617*, (Knopf, 1978).

THE GOLDEN AGE OF THE TANG
Fairbank, *op. cit.*
Huang, Ray, *China: A Macro History*, (An East Gate Book, 1988).
Keay, *op. cit.*
Lewis, Mark Edward, *China's Cosmopolitan Empire: The Tang Dynasty*, (Belknap Press of Harvard University Press, 2009).
Roberts, *op. cit.*

THE GLORIOUS SONG
Fairbank, *op. cit.*
Keay, *op. cit.*
Kuhn, Dieter, *The Age of Confucian Rule: The Song Transformation of China*, (Belknap Press of Harvard University Press, 2009).
Roberts, *op. cit.*

Wu, David, "Emperor Taizu of Song: Military Leader and Humanitarian Ruler," *The Epoch Times*, October 16-22, 2014.

Conquest and Unification by the Mongols
Brook, Timothy, *The Troubled Empire: China in the Yuan and Ming Dynasties*, (Belknap Press of Harvard University Press, 2010).
Dardess, John W., *Confucianism and Autocracy: Professional Elites in the Founding of the Ming Dynasty*, (University of California Press, 1983).
Fairbank, *op. cit.*
Gordon, Stewart, *When Asia Was the World*, (Da Capo Press, 2008).
Keay, *op. cit.*
Roberts, *op. cit.*

The Ming Dynasty, its Mighty Navy, and the Great Wall
Brook, *op. cit.*
Fairbank, *op. cit.*
Huang, *op. cit.*
Hung, Ho-fung, *Maritime Capitalism in Seventeenth-Century China: The Rise and Fall of Koxinga Revisited.* (John Hopkins University: http://irows.ucr.edu/papers/irows72/irows72.htm, 2000), accessed September 19, 2014.
Keay, *op. cit.*
Levanthes, Louise, *When China Ruled the Seas: The Treasure Fleet of the Dragon Throne, 1405-1433*, (Oxford University Press, 1996).
Parkes, Henry Bamford, *A History of Mexico*, (Houghton Mifflin Company, 1960)
Roberts, *op. cit.*

The Manchurian Qing Dynasty
Fairbank, *op. cit.*
Keay, *op. cit.*
Roberts, *op. cit.*
Rowe, William T., *China's Last Empire: The Great Qing*, (Belknap Press of Harvard University Press, 2009).

Sources

THE CORPORATE-INDUSTRIAL COLONIZATION OF CHINA
Bradley, James, *The China Mirage: The Hidden History of American Disaster in Asia*, (Little, Brown and Company, 2015).
Fairbank, *op. cit.*
Keay, *op. cit.*
Lovell, Julia, *The Opium War: Drugs, Dreams and the Making of China*, (The Overlook Press, 2011).
Meyer, Karl E., "The Opium War's Secret History," *The New York Times*, June 28, 1997.
Roberts, *op. cit.*
Rowe, *op. cit.*
Spence, Jonathan D., *The Search for Modern China*, (W. W. Norton, 2nd Ed. 1999)
Womack, Brantly, Ed., *China's Rise in Historical Perspective*, (Rowman & Littlefield, 2010).

A TROUBLING MATTER OF DIPLOMACY
Bradley, James, *The Imperial Cruise: A Secret History of Empire and War*, (Little, Brown and Company, 2009).
Maslin, Janet, *The Queasy Side of Theodore Roosevelt's Diplomatic Voyage*, (*New York Times*, November 18, 2009).
Hampson, Rick, *"Imperial Cruise" hits rough waters in attack of Roosevelt*, (*USATODAY*, November 24, 2009).
Oliver, Robert T., *Syngman Rhee: The Man Behind the Myth*, (Dodd Mead, 1955).
Spence, *op. cit.*
Treaty of Wanghia (complete text), http://en.wikisource.org/wiki/Treaty_of_Wanghia, accessed October 4, 2014.

PART TWO - THE COMMUNIST DYNASTY
DEATH THROES OF AN EMPIRE
Carr, Caleb, *The Devil Soldier: The American Soldier of Fortune Who Became a God in China*, (Random House, 1992)
Fairbank, *op. cit.*

Keay, *op. cit.*

Platt, Stephen R., *Autumn in the Heavenly Kingdom: China, the West, and the Epic Story of the Taiping Civil War*, (Vintage Books, 2012).

Preston, Diana, *The Boxer Rebellion: The Dramatic Story of China's War on Foreigners That Shook the World In the Summer of 1900*. (Walker, 2000).

Roberts, *op. cit.*

Silbey, David, *The Boxer Rebellion and the Great Game in China*, (Hill and Wang, 2012).

NATIONALISM AND THE REPUBLICAN REVOLUTION

Bailey, Paul J., *China in the Twentieth Century*, (Blackwell, 2nd Ed. 2001).

Boyle, John H., *China and Japan at War, 1937-1945: The Politics of Collaboration*, (Stanford University Press, 1972).

Bunker, Gerald E., *The Peace Conspiracy: Wang Ching-wei and the China War, 1937-1941*, (Harvard University Press, 1972).

Chang, Jung and Jon Halliday, *Mao, The Unknown Story*, (Anchor Books, 2005), was the primary source of Mao quotes.

Fairbank, *op. cit.*

Keay, *op. cit.*

Lawrence, Alan, *China Since 1919: Revolution and Reform: A Sourcebook* (Routledge, 2004).

Pantsov, Alexander and Steven I. Levine, *Mao: The Real Story*, (Simon & Schuster, 2012).

Roberts, *op. cit.*

Short, Philip, *Mao: A Life* (Henry Holt, 2000)

Spence, *op. cit.*

Thornton, Richard C., *China: The Struggle for Power, 1917-1972*, (Indiana University Press, 1972).

JAPANESE AGGRESSION

Brady, James, *Warning of War: A Novel of the North China Marines*, (Thomas Dunn Books, 2002).

Sources

Fairbank, *op. cit.*
Keay, *op. cit.*
Lindsay, Michael, *The Unknown War: North China, 1937-1945*, (Two Continents Publishing Group, 1977).
Mitter, Rana, *Forgotten Ally: China's World War II, 1937-1945*, (Houghton Mifflin Harcourt, 2013).
Pantsov and Levine, *op. cit.*
Roberts, *op. cit.*
Short, *op. cit.*
Spence, *op. cit.*
Thornton, *op. cit.*
Worthing, Peter M., *A Military History of Modern China: From the Manchu Conquest to Tian'anmen Square*, (Praeger Security International, 2007).

THE LONG MARCH

Chang and Halliday, *op. cit.* was the primary source of Mao quotes.
Fairbank, *op. cit.*
Keay, *op. cit.*
Lawrence, Anthony, *China: The Long March*, (Intercontinental Publishing Co., 1986).
Pantsov and Levine, *op. cit.*
Roberts, *op. cit.*
Salisbury, Harrison E., *The Long March: The Untold Story*, (Harper & Row, 1985).
Short, *op. cit.*
Sun, Shuyun, *The Long March: The True History of Communist China's Founding Myth*, (Doubleday 2006).
Thornton, *op. cit.*
Worthing, *op. cit.*
Mao, Zedong, *Quotations From Chairman Mao Tsetung*, (Foreign Language Press, 1976).

WORLD WAR

Chang and Halliday, *op. cit.* was the primary source of Mao quotes.
Davies, John P., Jr., *Dragon by the Tail: American, British, Japanese, and Russian Encounters with China and One Another*, (W. W. Norton, 1972).
Fairbank, *op. cit.*
Keay, *op. cit.*
Lindsay, *op. cit.*
Mitter, *op. cit.*
Pantsov and Levine, *op. cit.*
Roberts, *op. cit.*
Short, *op. cit.*
Thornton, *op. cit.*
Tuchman, Barbara Tuchman, *Stilwell and the American Experience in China, 1911–45* (Macmillan Co., 1971).
Worthing, *op. cit.*

MAO ESTABLISHES A DYNASTY

Chang and Halliday, *op. cit.* was the primary source of Mao quotes.
Fairbank, *op. cit.*
Heuston, Kimberley Burton, *Mao Zedong*, (Franklin Watts, 2010).
Keay, *op. cit.*
Li, Zhisui, *The Private Life of Chairman Mao: The Memoirs of Mao's Personal Physician*, (Chatto & Windus, 1994).
Orwell, George, *Animal Farm*, (Harcourt Brace Jovanovich, 1946).
Pantsov and Levine, *op. cit.*
Roberts, *op. cit.*
Short, *op. cit.* was the source of Mao quotes about sexuality.
Thornton, *op. cit.*
Zedong, *op. cit.*

MAO'S INSANE REIGN

Bailey, *op. cit.*
Chang and Halliday, *op. cit.* was the primary source of Mao quotes.
Fairbank, *op. cit.*

Sources

Heuston, *op. cit.*
Pantsov and Levine, *op. cit.*
Roberts, *op. cit.*
Short, *op. cit.*
Spence, *op. cit.*
Thornton, *op. cit.*
Worthing, *op. cit.*

DENG'S MODERATE RULE
Cormier, Michael, *The Legacy of Tiananmen Square*, (Goose Lane Editions, 2011) was the primary source of quotes about Tiananmen Square.
Denyer, Simon, "Horrors of one-child policy leave deep scars in Chinese society," *The Washington Post*, October 30, 2015.
Fairbank, *op. cit.*
Lampton, David M., *Following the Leader: Ruling China, From Deng Xiaoping to Xi Jinping*, (University of California Press, 2014)
Roberts, *op. cit.*
Vogel, Ezra F., *Deng Xiaoping and the Transformation of China*, (Belknap Press of Harvard University Press, 2011) was the primary source of Deng quotes.
Worthing, *op. cit.*

THE TIGER'S PRAGMATIC RULE
Associated Press in Beijing, "China Tries Seven Students on Separatist Charges," *The Guardian*, November 25, 2014.
Barboza, David, "Billions in Hidden Riches for Family of Chinese Leader," *The New York Times*, October 25, 2012.
Branagan, Tania, "Xi Jinping Vows to Fight 'Tigers' and 'Flies' in Anti-Corruption Drive, *The Guardian*, January 22, 2013.
Brown, Kerry, *Hu Jintao: China's Silent Ruler*, (World Scientific Publishing Company, 2012).
Buckley, Chris and Andrew Jacobs, "Maoists in China, Given New Life, Attack Dissent," *The New York Times*, January 4, 2015.
Cormier, *op. cit.*

Economist, The "China and the Environment: The East is Grey," August 10, 2013.

Forsythe, Michael, et. al., "Xi Jinping Millionaire Relations Reveal Fortunes of Elite," *Bloomberg News,* June 29, 2012.

Forsythe, Michael, "As China's Leader Fights Graft, His Relatives Shed Assets," *The New York Times,* June 17, 2014.

Gregory, Stephen, "After Long Buildup, China Announces Arrest of Former Security Tsar Zhou Yongkang," *The Epoch Times,* July 29, 2014.

---, "Jiang Zemin at Bay in Shanghai," *The Epoch Times,* August 19, 2014.

Hessler, Peter, "China: Inside the Dragon," *National Geographic,* May 2008.

Ho, Pin and Wenguang Huang, *A Death in the Lucky Holiday Hotel: Murder, Money, and an Epic Power Struggle in China*, (Public Affairs, 2013).

Huang, Cary, "China's Xi Jinping Supports 'Democracy'…but Not in the Western Sense," *South China Morning Post*, September 24, 2014.

Jacobs, Andrew and Chris Buckley, "Presumed Guilty in China's War on Corruption, Targets Suffer Abuses," *The New York Times*, October 19, 2014.

---, "In China, Civic Groups' Freedom, and Followers, Are Vanishing," *The New York Times*, February 26, 2015.

---, "Move Over Mao: Beloved 'Papa Xi' Awes China," *The New York Times*, March 7, 2015.

Jacobs, Andrew, "China Raids Offices of Rights Group as Crackdown on Activism Continues," *The New York Times*, March 26, 2015.

---, "Taking Feminist Battle to China's Streets, and Landing in Jail, *The New York Times*, April 5, 2015.

Jacobs, Andrew and Chris Buckley, "China Targeting Rights Lawyers in a Crackdown," *The New York Times,* July 22, 2015.

Kaiman, Jonathan, "China Gets Richer but More Unequal," *The Guardian*, July 28, 2014.

Sources

Kahn, Joseph and Jim Yardley, "As China Roars, Pollution Reaches Deadly Extremes," *The New York Times*, August 26, 2007.

Kilgour, David and David Matas, *Bloody Harvest: The Killing of Falun Gong for Their Organs*, (Seraphim Editions, 2009).

Kuhn, Robert Lawrence, *The Man Who Changed China: The Life and Legacy of Jiang Zemin*, (Crown, 2004).

Lim, Benjamin Kang and Ben Blanchard, "China Puts Former Security Chief Under House Arrest-Sources," *Reuters*, December 11, 2013.

Minter, Adam, "Xi's Cultural Revolution Looks Doomed To Fail," *The Japan Times*, December 8, 2014.

Phillips, Tom, "US Urged to Cancel Xi Jinping Visit After China's Human Rights Crackdown," *The Guardian*, July 14, 2015.

---, "Families of China's 'Disappeared' Say Country is a Place of Fear and Panic," *The Guardian*, August 31, 2015.

Sanderson, Henry, "China's Xi Amassing Most Power Since Deng Raises Reform Risk," *Bloomberg News*, December 30, 2013.

---, "Combat-Ready China Military Seen as Xi's Goal in Graft Battle," *Bloomberg News*, April 1, 2014.

Sharp, Jonathan, Ed., South China Morning Post, *The China Renaissance: The Rise of Xi Jinping and the 18th Communist Party Congress*, (World Scientific Publishing Company, 2013).

Shirk, Susan L., *China: Fragile Superpower: How China's Internal Politics Could Derail its Peaceful Rise*, (Oxford University Press, 2008).

Vogel, *op. cit.*

We, Sui-Lee, "China Jails Journalists for Severn Years for 'Leaking State Secrets,'" *Reuters*, April 17, 2015.

Wikipedia, *Xi Jinping*, http://en.wikipedia.org/wiki/Xi_Jinping, accessed October 13, 2014.

Woellert, Lorraine and Sharon Chen, "China's Income Inequality Surpasses U.S., Posing Risk for Xi," *Bloomberg News,* April 29, 2014.

Womack, *op. cit.*

Wong, Edward, "In New China, 'Hostile' West Is Still Derided," *The New York Times*, November 11, 2014.

---, "China Uses 'Picking Quarrels" Charge to cast a Wider Net Online," *The New York Times*, July 26, 2015.
Wright, Teresa, *Party and State in Post-Mao China (China Today)*, (Polity, 2015).
Wu, Zhong, "China Yearns for Hu's 'Harmonious Society,'" *Asia Times*, October 11, 2006.

PART THREE: CHINA AND THE UNITED STATES
Alexander, David, "U.S. Says China Has Placed Mobile Artillery on Reclaimed Island," *Reuters*, May 29, 2015.
Alterman, Eric, *What Liberal Media?*, (Basic Books, 2003).
Brunnstrom, David, "U.S. Vows to Continue Patrols After China Warns Spy Plane," *Reuters*, May 21, 2015.
Conason, Joe, *Big Lies: The Right-Wing Propaganda Machine and How it Distorts the Truth*, (Thomas Dunn Books, 2003).
Goodman, Amy, *The Exception to the Rulers: Exposing Oily Politicians, War Profiteers, and the Media That Love Them*, (Hyperion, 2001).
Govindasamy, Siva, "Vietnam Eyes Western Warplanes, Patrol Aircraft to Counter China," *Reuters*, June 5, 2015.
Greenberg, Eric H. and Karl Weber, *Generation We: How the Millennial Youth are Taking Over America and Changing Our World Forever*, (Pachatusan, 2008).
Hartmann, Thom, *Rebooting the American Dream: 11 Ways to Rebuild Our Country*, (Berrett-Koehler Publishers, 2010).
Hightower, James, *Thieves in High Places: They've Stolen Our Country— And It's Time to Take it Back*, (Viking, 2003).
Jacobs, Andrew, "China, Updating Military Strategy, Puts Focus on Projecting Naval Power, *The New York Times*, May 26, 2015.
Kelly, Tim, "U.S. to Bring Japan Under its Cyber Defense Umbrella," (*Reuters,* May 30, 2015).
Kuttner, Robert, *The Squandering of America: How the Failure of Our Politics Undermines Our Prosperity*, (Alfred A. Knopf, 2007).
Mao, *op. cit.*

Sources

Miller, Mark Crispin, *Fooled Again: The Real Case for Electoral Reform*, (Basic Books, 2005).

Palast, Greg, *The Best Democracy Money Can Buy*, (Plume, 2003)

Perlez, Jane, "Beijing, With an Eye on the South China Sea, Adds Patrol Ships," *The New York Times*, April 10, 2015.

Phillips, Kevin, *American Theocracy: The Peril and Politics of Radical Religion, Oil, and Borrowed Money in the 21st Century*, (Viking, 2006).

Phillips, Tom, "South China Sea: Beijing 'not frightened to fight a war' after US move," *The Guardian*, October 28, 2015.

Rich, Frank, *The Greatest Story Ever Sold: The Decline and Fall of Truth in Bush's America*, (Penguin, 2006)

Roosevelt Institution, The, *25 Ideas for Election Reform*, (Vol. 2, Issue 1, June 2008)

Ross, Carne, *The Leaderless Revolution: How Ordinary People Will Take Power and Change Politics in the 21st Century*, (Blue Rider Press, 2011).

Sanger, David E. and Rick Gladstone, "Piling Sand in a Disputed Sea, China Literally Gains Ground," *The New York Times*, April 8, 2015.

Smith, Hedrick, *Who Stole the American Dream*, (Random House, 2012).

Surowiecki, James, *The Wisdom of Crowds*, (Doubleday, 1967).

Taibbi, Matt, *Griftopia: A Story of Bankers, Politicians, and the Most Audacious Power Grab in American History*, (Spiegel & Grau, 2010).

Tasini, Jonathan, *The Audacity of Greed: Free Markets, Corporate Thieves, and the Looting of America*, (IG Publishing, 2009).

Thayer, Carl, "Analyzing the US-Philippines Enhanced Defense Cooperation Agreement," *The Diplomat*, May 2, 2014.

Epilogue

Baldwin, Claire, "Hong Kong Student Leaders Banned From Mong Kok Protest Site," *Reuters*, November 27, 2014.

Baldwin, Clare, Yimou Lee, and Clare Jim, "Special Report: The Mainland's Colonization of the Hong Kong Economy," *Reuters*, December 31, 2014.

Bradsher, Keith and Chris Buckley, "Beijing Is Directing Hong Kong Strategy, Government Insiders Say," *The New York Times*, October 17, 2014.

---, "Hong Kong Leader Reaffirms Unbending Stance on Elections," *The New York Times*, October 20, 2014.

Buckley, Chris and Alan Wong, "At 17, Setting Off Protests That Roil Hong Kong," *The New York Times*, October 2, 2014.

---, "Pro-Democracy Movement's Vote in Hong Kong Abruptly Called Off," *The New York Times*, October 26, 2014.

Buckley, Chris and Keith Bradsher, "Hong Kong Protesters Lose a Last Bastion, but Vow to Go On," *The New York Times*, December 11, 2014.

Ching, Frank, "Patriotism is Proving Hard to Define," *South China Morning Post*, August 12, 2014.

Chow, Jason, Enda Curran, and Isabella Steger, "Hong Kong Police Clear Part of Protest Site," *The Wall Street Journal*, October 17, 1014.

Denyer, Simon, "Beijing Reminds Hong Kong Residents That it Remains 'the Real Boss,'" *The Washington Post,* June 11, 2014.

Gough, Neil, "Hong Kong Wealth Gap on Display in Protests," *The New York Times,* October 6, 2014.

Jacobs, Andres, "Hong Kong Democracy Standoff, Circa 1960," *The New York Times*, October 27, 2014.

Kaiman, Jonathan, "Hong Kong's unofficial pro-democracy referendum irks Beijing," *The Guardian*, June 25, 2014.

---, "Hong Kong protests: 20 injured after second night of clashes," *The Guardian*, October 18, 2014.

---, "Hong Kong protesters shout 'shame on you' outside home of city chief," *The Guardian*, October 22, 2014.

Kwok, Donny and Diane Chan, "Thousands of Activists Stage 'Black Cloth' March in Hong Kong," *Reuters*, September 14, 2014.

---, "Hong Kong protesters march after fruitless talks with government," *Reuters*, October 22, 2014.

Sources

Law, Violet and Julie Makinen, "Police Unleash Tear Gas as Democracy Protests Escalate in Hong Kong," *Los Angeles Times*, September 28, 2014.

Lee, Peter R., "The Unelected Battle the Selected: Democracy in Hong Kong," *China Matters*, October 22, 2014, http://chinamatters.blogspot.com/2014/10/the-unelected-battle-selected-democracy.html, accessed October 23, 2014.

Chen, Pokong, "Ten Ways to Understand Hong Kong's Occupy Central," *The Epoch Times*, October 23-29, 2014.

Pomfret, James, "China Asserts Paternal Rights Over Hong Kong in Democracy Clash," *Reuters*, September 11, 2014.

Pomfret, James and Elzio Barreto, "Hong Kong democracy street battles rage on despite imminent talks," *Reuters*, October 18, 2014.

Sala, Ilaria Maria, Tania Branigan, and Jonathan Kaiman, "Hong Kong Police Drive Out Pro-democracy Protesters in Violent Clashes," *The Guardian*, December 1, 2014.

Shan, Kao, "Key Hong Kong Pro-democracy Students Charged After Occupy Protests," *Reuters*, August 19, 2015.

Sun, Qixiao, "China's State-Run Media Mum on Chinese Premier's Views on Hong Kong," *The Epoch Times,* October 16-22, 2014.

Ruwitch, John, "Police Reputation and Morale at Stake in Hong Kong Protests," *Reuters*, November 2, 2014.

Wikipedia, "Hong Kong,""2014 Hong Kong Electoral Reform," and "2014 Hong Kong Protests," accessed October 17, 2014.

William John Cox

For more than 45 years, William John Cox has written extensively on law, politics, philosophy, and the human condition. During that time, he vigorously pursued a career in law enforcement, public policy, and the law.

As a police officer, Cox was an early leader in the "New Breed" movement to professionalize law enforcement. He wrote the *Policy Manual* of the Los Angeles Police Department and the introductory chapters of the *Police Task Force Report* of the National Advisory Commission on Criminal Justice Standards and Goals, which continues to define the role of the police in America.

As an attorney, Cox worked for the U.S. Department of Justice to implement national standards and goals, prosecuted cases for the Los Angeles County District Attorney's Office, and operated a public interest law practice primarily dedicated to the defense of young people.

He wrote notable law review articles and legal briefs in major cases, tried a number of jury trials, and argued cases in the superior and appellate courts that made law.

Professionally, Cox volunteered *pro bono* services in several landmark legal cases. In 1979, he filed a class-action lawsuit on behalf of all citizens directly in the U.S. Supreme Court alleging that the government no longer represented the voters who elected it. As a remedy, Cox urged the Court to require national policy referendums to be held in conjunction with presidential elections.

In 1981, representing a Jewish survivor of Auschwitz, Cox investigated and successfully sued a group of radical right-wing organizations which denied the Holocaust. The case was the subject of the Turner Network Television motion picture, *Never Forget*.

Cox later represented a secret client and arranged the publication of almost 1,800 photographs of ancient manuscripts that had been kept from the public for more than 40 years. *A Facsimile Edition of the Dead Sea Scrolls* was published in November 1991. His role in that effort is described by historian Neil Asher Silberman in *The Hidden Scrolls: Christianity, Judaism, and the War for the Dead Sea Scrolls*.

Cox concluded his legal career as a Supervising Trial Counsel for the State Bar of California. There, he led a team of attorneys and investigators which prosecuted attorneys accused of serious misconduct and criminal gangs engaged in the illegal practice of law. He retired in 2007.

Continuing to concentrate on policy, political, and social issues since his retirement, Cox has lectured, taught classes at the university level, produced a series of articles and books, moderated several Internet websites, and maintained an extensive worldwide correspondence. He can be contacted through his website at www.williamjohncox.com.

www.ingramcontent.com/pod-product-compliance
Lightning Source LLC
Chambersburg PA
CBHW061942070426
42450CB00007BA/940